CW01521688

Time Management

Time Management

Edited by
Pierre Moreau

www.larsen-keller.com

Time Management
Edited by Pierre Moreau
ISBN: 978-1-63549-671-0 (Hardback)

© 2018 Larsen & Keller

 Larsen & Keller

Published by Larsen and Keller Education,
5 Penn Plaza,
19th Floor,
New York, NY 10001, USA

Cataloging-in-Publication Data

Time management / edited by Pierre Moreau.
    p. cm.
Includes bibliographical references and index.
ISBN 978-1-63549-671-0
1. Time management. 2. Time. 3. Personal information management.
I. Moreau, Pierre.
HD69.T54 T56 2018
650.11--dc23

This book contains information obtained from authentic and highly regarded sources. All chapters are published with permission under the Creative Commons Attribution Share Alike License or equivalent. A wide variety of references are listed. Permissions and sources are indicated; for detailed attributions, please refer to the permissions page. Reasonable efforts have been made to publish reliable data and information, but the authors, editors and publisher cannot assume any responsibility for the vailidity of all materials or the consequences of their use.

Trademark Notice: All trademarks used herein are the property of their respective owners. The use of any trademark in this text does not vest in the author or publisher any trademark ownership rights in such trademarks, nor does the use of such trademarks imply any affiliation with or endorsement of this book by such owners.

For more information regarding Larsen and Keller Education and its products, please visit the publisher's website www.larsen-keller.com

Table of Contents

Preface

Managing time efficiently is a skill. The key to time management is to utilize time effectively so that there is no wastage. Keeping a clear vision or goal to be achieved provides motivation and focus to finish tasks. Step-by-step planning, prioritizing, creating a schedule or planner are simple ways to keep track of goals and to review one's progress. This book provides significant information of this area to help develop a good understanding of time management. It is appropriate for students seeking detailed information in this area.

To facilitate a deeper understanding of the contents of this book a short introduction of every chapter is written below:

Chapter 1- Managing time is an important asset in our age. Professional, academic and even household activities require good management of time. Prioritizing, organizing and keeping track of achievable goals are important ways of managing time. This chapter provides an overview of time management.

Chapter 2- Creating time schedules and planners are good ways to manage time effectively. Timetables help to focus on a task as well as relax and reinvigorate oneself when required. Planners help keep track of time and evaluate efficiency. This chapter discusses the methods of time management as well as provides key analysis to the subject matter.

Chapter 3- In certain professions, time management is a fundamental requirement. Leading a team or a project requires planning and computation of potential time that would be needed to finish a task. Multi-tasking and preparing a to-do list are basic ways to tackle effective management of time. The major aspects related to daily time management are dealt with great details in the chapter. It provides a step-by-step account of achieving these routines as well.

Chapter 4- Careful organization of tasks is important in short-term as well as long-term activities. Organizing and prioritizing tasks make them easier to accomplish. Effective time management helps to meet set deadlines and accomplish them. This chapter elucidates ways to organize time wisely.

Chapter 5- Procrastination hampers an individual's efficiency. Focusing on goals, staying motivated and avoiding distractions are effective techniques to avoid procrastination. The aspects elucidated in this chapter are of vital importance to provide a better understanding of time management.

Chapter 6- Productivity is very important for achieving goals on time. Techniques to improve productivity include avoiding procrastination, breaking down tasks for easier management and staying orga-nized. Time management is best understood in confluence with the major topics that have been listed in the following chapter.

Chapter 7- Time allocation is an important aspect in achieving goals. Working under a deadline requires strict allocation of time for completion of tasks. Techniques and software available that can evaluate the time spent on tasks are explained in this chapter.

Finally, I would like to thank the entire team involved in the inception of this book for their valuable time and contribution. This book would not have been possible without their efforts. I would also like to thank my friends and family for their constant support.

Editor

Time Management Essentials

Managing time is an important asset in our age. Professional, academic and even household activities require good management of time. Prioritizing, organizing and keeping track of achievable goals are important ways of managing time. This chapter provides an overview of time management.

Time Management

Time management is the process of planning and exercising conscious control over the amount of time spent on specific activities, especially to increase effectiveness, efficiency or productivity.

It is a meta-activity with the goal to maximize the overall benefit of a set of other activities within the boundary condition of a limited amount of time, as time itself cannot be managed because it is fixed.

Time management may be aided by a range of skills, tools, and techniques used to manage time when accomplishing specific tasks, projects, and goals complying with a due date. Initially, time management referred to just business or work activities, but eventually the term broadened to include personal activities as well. A time management system is a designed combination of processes, tools, techniques, and methods. Time management is usually a necessity in any project development as it determines the project completion time and scope.

The major themes arising from the literature on time management include the following:

- Creating an environment conducive to effectiveness

- Setting of priorities

- Carrying out activity around prioritization.

- The related process of reduction of time spent on non-priorities

- Incentives to modify behavior to ensure compliance with time-related deadlines.

Time management is related to different concepts such as:

- Project management: Time Management can be considered to be a project management subset and is more commonly known as project planning and project scheduling. Time Management has also been identified as one of the core functions identified in project management.

- Attention management: Attention Management relates to the management of cognitive resources, and in particular the time that humans allocate their mind (and organize the minds of their employees) to conduct some activities.

Organizational Time Management is the science of identifying, valuing and reducing wasted time within organizations. Organizational Time Management identifies, reports and financially values sustainable time, wasted time and productive time within an organization and develops the business case to convert wasted time into productive time through the funding of products, services, projects or initiatives at a positive return on investment.

Creating an Effective Environment

Some time-management literature stresses tasks related to the creation of an environment conducive to "real" effectiveness. These strategies include principles such as:

- "get organized" - the triage of paperwork and of tasks

- "protecting one's time" by insulation, isolation and delegation

- "achievement through goal-management and through goal-focus" - motivational emphasis

- "recovering from bad time-habits" - recovery from underlying psychological problems, e.g. procrastination

Writers on creating an environment for effectiveness refer to such matters as having a tidy office or home for unleashing creativity, and the need to protect "prime time". Literature also focuses on overcoming chronic psychological issues such as procrastination.

Excessive and chronic inability to manage time effectively may result from Attention Deficit Hyperactivity Disorder (ADHD) or Attention Deficit Disorder (ADD). Diagnostic criteria include a sense of underachievement, difficulty getting organized, trouble getting started, many projects going simultaneously and trouble with follow-through. Some authors focus on the prefrontal cortex which is the most recently evolved part of the brain. It controls the functions of attention-span, impulse-control, organization, learning from experience and self-monitoring, among others. Some authors argue that changing the way the prefrontal cortex works is possible and offer a solution.

Setting Priorities and Goals

Time management strategies are often associated with the recommendation to set personal goals. The literature stresses themes such as -

- "Work in Priority Order" - set goals and prioritize

- "Set gravitational goals" - that attract actions automatically

These goals are recorded and may be broken down into a project, an action plan, or a simple task list. For individual tasks or for goals, an importance rating may be established, deadlines may be set, and priorities assigned. This process results in a plan with a task list or a schedule or calendar of activities. Authors may recommend a daily, weekly, monthly or other planning periods associated with different scope of planning or review. This is done in various ways, as follows.

ABC Analysis

A technique that has been used in business management for a long time is the categorization of large data into groups. These groups are often marked A, B, and C—hence the name. Activities are ranked by these general criteria:

- A – Tasks that are perceived as being urgent and important,
- B – Tasks that are important but not urgent,
- C – Tasks that are unimportant. (whether urgent or not)

Each group is then rank-ordered by priority. To further refine the prioritization, some individuals choose to then force-rank all "B" items as either "A" or "C". ABC analysis can incorporate more than three groups.

ABC analysis is frequently combined with Pareto analysis.

Pareto Analysis

This is the idea 80% of tasks can be completed in 20% of the disposable time. The remaining 20% of tasks will take up 80% of the time. This principle is used to sort tasks into two parts. According to this form of Pareto analysis it is recommended that tasks that fall into the first category be assigned a higher priority.

The 80-20-rule can also be applied to increase productivity: it is assumed that 80% of the productivity can be achieved by doing 20% of the tasks. Similarly, 80% of results can be attributed to 20% of activity. If productivity is the aim of time management, then these tasks should be prioritized higher.

It depends on the method adopted to complete the task. There is always a simpler and easier way to complete the task. If one uses a complex way, it will be time consuming. So, one should always try to find out alternative ways to complete each task.

The Eisenhower Method

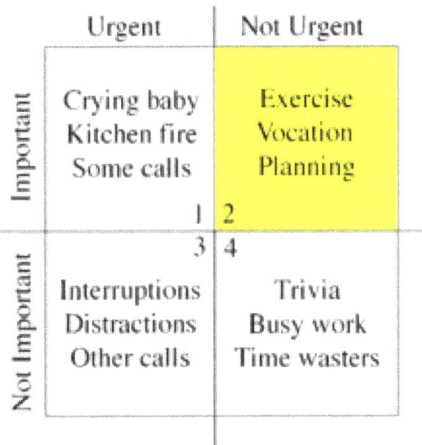

A basic "Eisenhower box" to help evaluate urgency and importance.
Items may be placed at more precise points within each quadrant.

The "Eisenhower Method" stems from a quote attributed to Dwight D. Eisenhower: "I have two kinds of problems, the urgent and the important. The urgent are not important, and the important are never urgent."

Using the Eisenhower Decision Principle, tasks are evaluated using the criteria important/unimportant and urgent/not urgent, and then placed in according quadrants in an Eisenhower Matrix (also known as an "Eisenhower Box" or "Eisenhower Decision Matrix"). Tasks are then handled as follows:

Tasks in

1. Important/Urgent quadrant are done immediately and personally e.g. crises, deadlines, problems.

2. Important/Not Urgent quadrant get an end date and are done personally e.g. relationships, planning, recreation.

3. Unimportant/Urgent quadrant are delegated e.g. interruptions, meetings, activities.

4. Unimportant/Not Urgent quadrant are dropped e.g. time wasters, pleasant activities, trivia.

This method is said to have been used by U.S. President Dwight D. Eisenhower.

Domino Reaction Method

This is the idea that there are actions that you invest in once and which produce over time in different channels. Writing a book is such an action, because it requires a one-time effort, and once you finish it, it continues serving you.

POSEC Method

POSEC is an acronym for *Prioritize by Organizing, Streamlining, Economizing and Contributing*. The method dictates a template which emphasizes an average individual's immediate sense of emotional and monetary security. It suggests that by attending to one's personal responsibilities first, an individual is better positioned to shoulder collective responsibilities.

Inherent in the acronym is a hierarchy of self-realization, which mirrors Abraham Maslow's hierarchy of needs:

1. Prioritize - Your time and define your life by goals.

2. Organize - Things you have to accomplish regularly to be successful (family and finances).

3. Streamline - Things you may not like to do, but must do (work and chores).

4. Economize - Things you should do or may even like to do, but they're not pressingly urgent (pastimes and socializing).

5. Contribute - By paying attention to the few remaining things that make a difference (social obligations).

Implementation of Goals

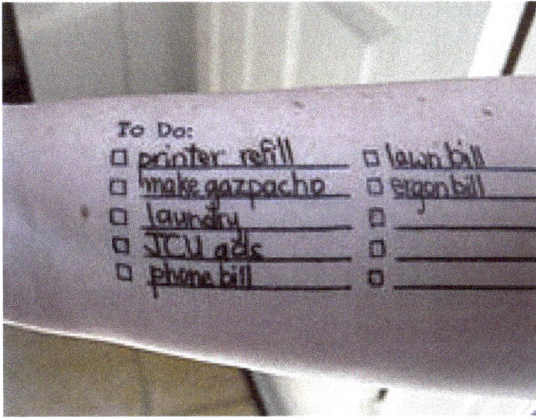

A to-do form tattooed into a person's arm, with some items already written out with a black pen.

A task list (also *to-do list* or *things-to-do*) is a list of tasks to be completed, such as chores or steps toward completing a project. It is an inventory tool which serves as an alternative or supplement to memory.

Task lists are used in self-management, grocery lists, business management, project management, and software development. It may involve more than one list.

When one of the items on a task list is accomplished, the task is checked or crossed off. The traditional method is to write these on a piece of paper with a pen or pencil, usually on a note pad or clip-board. Task lists can also have the form of paper or software checklists.

Writer Julie Morgenstern suggests "do's and don'ts" of time management that include:

- Map out everything that is important, by making a task list

- Create "an oasis of time" for one to control

- Say "No"

- Set priorities

- Don't drop everything

- Don't think a critical task will get done in one's spare time.

Numerous digital equivalents are now available, including Personal information management (PIM) applications and most PDAs. There are also several web-based task list applications, many of which are free.

Task list organization

Task lists are often tiered. The simplest tiered system includes a general to-do list (or task-holding file) to record all the tasks the person needs to accomplish, and a daily to-do list which is created each day by transferring tasks from the general to-do list.

Task lists are often prioritized:

- A daily list of things to do, numbered in the order of their importance, and done in that order one at a time until daily time allows, is attributed to consultant Ivy Lee (1877–1934) as the most profitable advice received by Charles M. Schwab (1862–1939), president of the Bethlehem Steel Corporation.

- An early advocate of "ABC" prioritization was Alan Lakein, in 1973. In his system "A" items were the most important ("A-1" the most important within that group), "B" next most important, "C" least important.

- A particular method of applying the *ABC method* assigns "A" to tasks to be done within a day, "B" a week, and "C" a month.

- To prioritize a daily task list, one either records the tasks in the order of highest priority, or assigns them a number after they are listed ("1" for highest priority, "2" for second highest priority, etc.) which indicates in which order to execute the tasks. The latter method is generally faster, allowing the tasks to be recorded more quickly.

- Another way of prioritizing compulsory tasks (group A) is to put the most unpleasant one first. When it's done, the rest of the list feels easier. Groups B and C can benefit from the same idea, but instead of doing the first task (which is the most unpleasant) right away, it gives motivation to do other tasks from the list to avoid the first one.

- A completely different approach which argues *against* prioritising altogether was put forward by British author Mark Forster in his book "Do It Tomorrow and Other Secrets of Time Management". This is based on the idea of operating "closed" to-do lists, instead of the traditional "open" to-do list. He argues that the traditional never-ending to-do lists virtually guarantees that some of your work will be left undone. This approach advocates getting all your work done, every day, and if you are unable to achieve it helps you diagnose where you are going wrong and what needs to change.

Various writers have stressed potential difficulties with to-do lists such as the following:

- Management of the list can take over from implementing it. This could be caused by procrastination by prolonging the planning activity. This is akin to analysis paralysis. As with any activity, there's a point of diminishing returns.

- Some level of detail must be taken for granted for a task system to work. Rather than put "clean the kitchen", "clean the bedroom", and "clean the bathroom", it is more efficient to put "housekeeping" and save time spent writing and reduce the system's administrative load (each task entered into the system generates a cost in time and effort to manage it, aside from the execution of the task). The risk of consolidating tasks, however, is that "housekeeping" in this example may prove overwhelming or nebulously defined, which will either increase the risk of procrastination, or a mismanaged project.

- Listing routine tasks wastes time. If you are in the habit of brushing your teeth every day, then there is no reason to put it down on the task list. The same goes for getting out of bed, fixing meals, etc. If you need to track routine tasks, then a standard list or chart may be useful, to avoid the procedure of manually listing these items over and over.

- To remain flexible, a task system must allow for disaster. A company must be ready for a disaster. Even if it is a small disaster, if no one made time for this situation, it can metastasize, potentially causing damage to the company.

- To avoid getting stuck in a wasteful pattern, the task system should also include regular (monthly, semi-annual, and annual) planning and system-evaluation sessions, to weed out inefficiencies and ensure the user is headed in the direction he or she truly desires.

- If some time is not regularly spent on achieving long-range goals, the individual may get stuck in a perpetual holding pattern on short-term plans, like staying at a particular job much longer than originally planned.

Software Applications

Many companies use time tracking software to track an employee's working time, billable hours etc., e.g. law practice management software.

Many software products for time management support multiple users. They allow the person to give tasks to other users and use the software for communication.

Task list applications may be thought of as lightweight personal information manager or project management software.

Modern task list applications may have built-in task hierarchy (tasks are composed of subtasks which again may contain subtasks), may support multiple methods of filtering and ordering the list of tasks, and may allow one to associate arbitrarily long notes for each task.

In contrast to the concept of allowing the person to use multiple filtering methods, at least one software product additionally contains a mode where the software will attempt to dynamically determine the best tasks for any given moment.

Time Management Systems

Time management systems often include a time clock or web-based application used to track an employee's work hours. Time management systems give employers insights into their workforce, allowing them to see, plan and manage employees' time. Doing so allows employers to control labor costs and increase productivity. A time management system automates processes, which eliminates paper work and tedious tasks.

GTD (Getting Things Done)

GTD Getting Things Done was created by David Allen and the basic idea behind this method is to finish all the small tasks immediately and a big task is to be divided into smaller tasks to start completing now. The reasoning behind this is to avoid the information overload or "brain freeze" which is likely to occur when there are hundreds of tasks. The thrust of GTD is to encourage the user to get their tasks and ideas out and on paper and organized as quickly as possible so they're easy to manage and see.

Pomodoro

Francesco Cirillo's "Pomodoro Technique" was originally conceived in the late 1980s and gradually refined until it was later defined in 1992. The technique is the namesake of a pomodoro (Italian for tomato) shaped kitchen timer initially used by Cirillo during his time at university. The "Pomodoro" is described as the fundamental metric of time within the technique and is traditionally defined as being 30 minutes long, consisting of 25 minutes of work and 5 minutes of break time. Cirillo also recommends a longer break of 15 to 30 minutes after every four Pomodoros. Through experimentation involving various work groups and mentoring activities, Cirillo determined the "ideal Pomodoro" to be 20–35 minutes long.

Elimination of Non-priorities

Time management also covers how to eliminate tasks that do not provide value to the individual or organization.

According to Sandberg, task lists "aren't the key to productivity [that] they're cracked up to be". He reports an estimated "30% of listers spend more time managing their lists than [they do] completing what's on them".

Hendrickson asserts that rigid adherence to task lists can create a "tyranny of the to-do list" that forces one to "waste time on unimportant activities".

How to Manage your Time

These days, time seems to be at a premium. We have devices that keep us constantly connected with work, with friends and family, and sometimes even with complete strangers. As a result, it is easy to get distracted. If you're like most of us, you have a lot to accomplish. We'll show you a great way to do just that!

Steps

1. Make a list of the tasks you need to accomplish. But before you can manage your time, you need to know what it is you must manage. A list of tasks, from the mundane to the critical, will help you get a handle on what needs to get done.

- Assign realistic priorities to each task:

    - Priority 1: due today by 6pm

    - Priority 2: due tomorrow by 6pm

    - Priority 3: due by the end of the week

    - Priority 4: due during next week

- You can further prioritize tasks within this grouping by adding a decimal place. For example, a Priority 1.0 task needs to be done immediately, whereas a Priority 1.5 task simply needs to be done by the end of day.

2. Balance your effort. Work on small portions every day of work that will be due by the end of the week, starting with the most important tasks first.

- Do today's tasks. Concentrate On what is at hand, do not allow yourself to lose focus. Then move on to the next daily task. Once today's tasks are completed, mark them as such, and proceed to tomorrow's tasks.

- When tomorrow's tasks are complete, work on the other tasks due by the end of the week, and when those are complete, work on the tasks due early next week. A small portion of each is better than one huge,laborious task and will keep your time managed more efficiently and reduce stress and eliminate burn-out.

- Make one of your final daily tasks the completion of *tomorrow's* task list. Each day should be ended with a new task sheet for tomorrow to keep you on track.

3. Focus on your most productive time of day. Some people work better in the morning, and some are more focused in the evening.

4. Manage time in increments. Play a game with yourself by competing against the clock.

- Work in fifteen minute, half hour or hour intervals,scientifically it is known that 45 minutes work followed by a 10 minutes rest is the best for the average student.
- Give yourself a time goal to complete a portion of a task or the entire task.

5. Take a break. Clear your mind and refresh yourself to refocus.

- Decide beforehand on a 5, 10 or 15 minute break and stick to that decision.
- Breaks provide incentive by giving you something to look forward to having.

6. Keep track of your progress.

- Cross things off the list as they are completed.
- You'll feel more relieved and relaxed just by getting through the daily tasks. Not only will you be getting things done, finishing tasks will give you a sense of accomplishment and spur motivation.

7. Reassess the list. Rewrite and prioritize your list on a regular basis.

- Add new tasks to the list. This should be done on a daily basis, especially when you are just getting started with a time management regimen.

- Eliminate or adjust tasks that are completed, or fall in priority.

- Delegate tasks to others. Contrary to popular belief, you don't need to do it all. You can be much more effective if you can delegate tasks as necessary.

- Use technology to complete tasks more quickly, efficiently or accurately. Today's mobile technology features dozens, if not hundreds of apps that will help you manage—and even accomplish—your tasks efficiently.

8. Leave time for fun. While there are times when we just need to power through a large project, it's important to give yourself time to let loose. Not only will it refresh your mind, it's good for your body, too. It doesn't have to be a lot of time but make sure that you do!

9. Sleep for 7-8 hours every night. Getting the proper amount of sleep will help keep you alert and energetic, able to think clearly, and function at a high level.

How to Develop your Sense of Time

Are you one of those people who, when asked how long ago something happened or how long something took, you give a rough estimate that's *way* off? Or are you chronically late because you're convinced that your morning routine or commute takes 15 minutes when in reality, it takes 25 or 30? Do you cook a dish for 50 minutes rather than 30 (as the recipe instructed) because you "lost track of time"? Some people are better able to judge the passing of time than others, but fortunately, this is an ability that can be developed with the following exercises.

Steps

1. Keep all your clocks as correct as you can make them. Remember to check the ones on your computer, car, and cell phone. When you enter a new environment, check any clocks and note whether or not they match yours. While you are training yourself, wear a watch or carry a phone or other clock with you at all times. The more accurate your clocks, the better you'll be able to fine-tune your sense of time.

2. Stabilize your circadian rhythm. Humans have a natural internal clock that regulates biological processes. If this rhythm is disrupted, not only will you have difficulty judging time, but it can also have negative effects on your health and productivity. To keep your circadian rhythm optimized, develop a routine in which you eat, sleep, and expose yourself to natural light at about the same times each day.

3. Every time you think of it, guess to yourself what time it is. Check a clock or watch. Make a point of correcting yourself. Think or say to yourself something like "I thought it was 10:20, but it's actually 10:34. I was 14 minutes slow." This is your time sense gap.

- You can make it a habit to do this every time you encounter a certain landmark or object, such as a stop sign, traffic light or mirror.

- You may want to try guessing the time when you awaken, if you do not wake to an alarm.

4. Whenever you get a chance, check a clock and make note of the time. Go about your regular life, attempting to guess when it has been one hour. Check a clock on your guess and make note of your time sense gap. As you get better, vary the time intervals you try to guess.

5. When you start a task with a defined beginning and end (reading a chapter of a book, driving to a friend's house, taking a shower) *guess how long it will take you.* When you finish, guess how

long it actually took you. Check the time. How far off was your initial guess? How far off was your second guess?

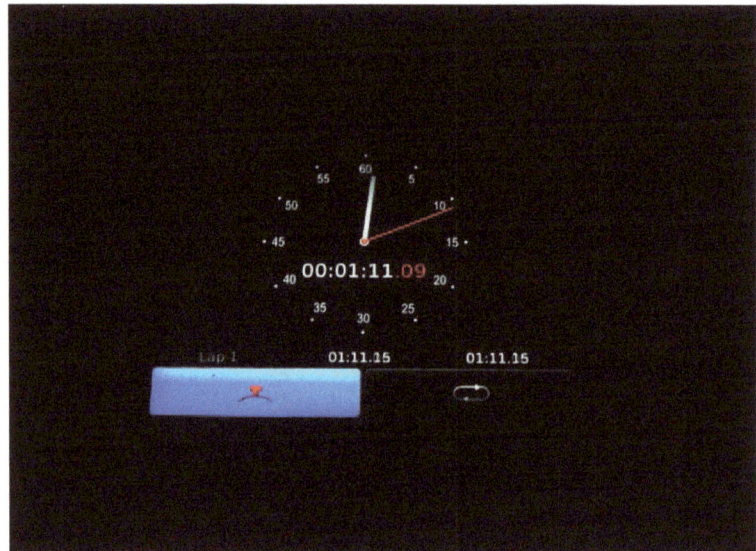

6. When you start a task that has a specified time frame (like when cooking), set a timer for the upper end of the range given. For example, if you're to cook oatmeal for 3-5 minutes, set a timer for 5 minutes. Assign yourself the task of guessing when 3 or 4 minutes have passed. If you make a mistake, the timer will save you from having burnt oatmeal. But with practice, you'll develop a sense for how long to leave the oatmeal cooking, as many chefs learn to do with various dishes they cook often.

7. Record your progress in a time sense journal. Whenever you observe a time sense gap, write it down. You might notice a pattern, like that you tend to be about 15 minutes slow in the morning, and 30 minutes fast in the afternoon. Or, like most people, time will seem to pass slowly when you're doing something monotonous or boring, and pass quickly when you're keeping busy or having fun. As you continue matching your guesses with reality, your sense of time will noticeably improve.

How to Improve Time Management Skills

It is difficult to get work done, meet deadlines, and be productive if you do not have good time management skills. Luckily, these are skills that you can work on and improve. The foundation of good time management includes organization and setting yourself up for success.

Method 1

Finding the Areas that Need Improvement

1. Keep a time diary. You may wonder where all of your time goes each day. Carry a notebook around and write down everything you do and for how long. You may be surprised about how you spend your time. Be honest when you do this.

- Try keeping a diary for at least a few days to get a good picture of how you typically spend your day. For example, going to a birthday dinner or a doctor's appointment is not an everyday task for you and could throw your schedule off.

2. Write down all the ways you waste time. There are many ways that you can waste time. Do you spend a lot of time on social media? Do you hang out with your friends when you should be doing other things? Do you spend hours in front of the television?

- It is important that you know yourself and your habits so you can make changes.

- Look through your time inventory and see areas that you can cut back on.

3. Determine why you procrastinate. Instead of becoming upset that you are putting a task off, try to figure out the reasons for your procrastination. Think of procrastinating as a symptom of a larger problem and try to get to the root cause. Are you scared to do the task? Are you tired? Is the task boring? Is the task too easy or too hard?

- If the task is too easy, offer yourself little rewards for completing each step.

- If the task is too hard, deadlines and small steps are the best way to tackle it.

- Take into consideration the amount of time you spend procrastinating as well when you do your time diary.

Method 2

Getting Organized

1. Make lists. Make lists of everything you plan on doing that day or that week. Once you're done, cross those things out so that you feel encouraged and motivated. Your list should be realistic and

attainable. If you make a list of 20 items but only achieve 5 items on your list, you will feel like you didn't get anything done.

- Prioritize your tasks so you know what's most important and needs to be completed first.

- If your list is too long, try having separate lists for different areas of your life such as personal, school/work, and home.

- People are typically more productive in the morning. Try to complete a more difficult task from your list in the morning and then handle the other items on your list. You will feel accomplished and can carry that momentum into the rest of your day.

2. Have deadlines. Your list only works if you actually use it. Setting deadlines will hold you accountable. Do your best to stick to your deadlines. Also be sure to set realistic deadlines that consider your responsibilities and other obligations.

- For example, if you need to schedule some personal appointments but will be tied up at meetings during work all day, a realistic deadline would be scheduling all of the appointments in the next few days instead of by the end of your busy work day.

- Give yourself some room for error when choosing a deadline. The deadline should be a few days before your task has to be finished.

3. Set reminders. You can set alarms on your phone, computer, or place visual reminders of the things you have to get done. Use the method that works best for you. It may help to use multiple

methods as well. Your reminders should be set for the final deadline and any mini deadlines to keep you on schedule.

- For example, if you have a task that needs to be completed in 2 weeks, you may have reminders set at day 7, day 10, and day 14.

4. Make use of a calendar. Systematize all your daily tasks so you can manage your time efficiently. Always check your calendar at the start of the day and make any necessary changes, so you know all your tasks for the day. Make sure your calendar is easily accessible and highlights all important events.

5. Plan during your downtime. You experience downtime throughout your day. You can use that time to make a quick list or set your priorities for the day. Commuting to work/school is an ideal time to get some of this planning done.

- All of your downtime should not be devoted to planning and organizing. This could become stressful and do more harm than good.

- If you have 10 minutes of downtime, start by devoting 2 or 3 minutes to getting organized.

Method 3

Being Productive

1. Do not multitask. You may think you are getting more done if you try to juggle a few things at once. However, doing too many things at once, you never give a single task your complete focus and attention. You will be more efficient if you devote all of your energy to complete a task before you move on to the next.

- For example, instead of answering emails and returning phone calls at the same time; answer all of your emails before you make phone calls.

- Switching back and forth between tasks is more work for your brain and slows down the process.

2. Delegate responsibilities if you can. You cannot do everything yourself. Allowing another person to take care of something allows you to devote yourself to another task while still getting everything done. Be sure you delegate to someone that is reliable and trustworthy. You do not want to waste time worrying if the person will get things done.

- Remember that delegating is a sign of strength and intelligence not weakness.

3. Get rid of distractions. You will complete a task more quickly if you can give it your full attention. Turn off any distractions such as email notifications, your phone, television, social media. Set aside time when you do not want to be disturbed and do not address any interruptions unless you have to.

- For example, if you plan to write or read something for 45 minutes, do not answer your phone or respond to any emails during this time. If you turn off the notifications, you will not even notice that people are trying to get in contact with you. Once the 45 minutes are up, you can check your email.

- Social media is a big distraction. Schedule social media time throughout the day and stay away from it unless it is during a scheduled time block.

4. Take breaks. You cannot work or be productive 24 hours a day. Schedule breaks throughout your day. A break will allow you to recharge and come back to a task with a fresh perspective. During a scheduled break you may:

- Get on social media
- Call a friend
- Take a walk
- Try to do something on your break that is completely unrelated to your task.

5. Give yourself incentives. At the start of a task that you don't really feel like doing, promise yourself a reward at the end of it. For example, if you have a writing assignment you need to complete but are in no mood to do, allow yourself to use Instagram for half an hour or less once you're done with the assignment.

- Make sure your reward is something that you really enjoy.
- Your reward should never cause a setback or cause you to get off track.

6. Avoid over-scheduling. It is easy to take on more than you can handle or believe that you can accomplish a task in a shorter amount of time. Try to be realistic and schedule only those things which you think you can achieve in an allocated amount of time. Also, try not to take on a lot of extra work.

- Learn to say "no" if you are already too busy. If you cannot say no, be honest about your time constraints. For example, if someone asks you to get something done by the end of the day, you may say, "I'm a little overloaded right now, but I can have it to you by the end of tomorrow."
- Over-scheduling can also lead to stress. When you are stressed, you become less productive.

7. Evaluate your schedule. At the end of each day, take a look at your list. If you did not accomplish everything on your list, what could you have done differently? What things did you do well? Adjust your schedule based on your evaluation.

- It will take time to find the best strategies for you. Maybe phone reminders work well, but planning during your downtime makes you super stressed.

How to Manage Time and Prioritise Work

Finding the time to do all you need in a day can be tough if you're unsure how to prioritise tasks. Too often we spend large amounts of time on tasks that have little impact when we should be putting all our energy into the tasks that are most valuable. We can often be busy without actually getting anything done, and this is where the art of preparation comes into play.

Creating tasks and achievable goals for ourselves can help us manage our time much more productively, while ranking tasks in the order of value and importance means that we can prioritise work effectively. Help organise your time and prioritise your work with this invaluable guide.

Steps

1. Set Goals you can Achieve. You need to be able to break the day's tasks into achievable targets that give you a clear sense of purpose. Keep the bigger picture in mind, i.e. what are you working to achieve? Have this goal as a clear vision, and use it to keep you focused on the work at hand.

2. Prioritise your Goals. Decide early on what the most valuable use of your time is. Evaluate how important each task is to you by weighing up their urgency against their value. If there any deadlines looming then be sure to focus on these first. Be sure to give yourself plenty of time to complete each task so you don't feel pressured or rushed when carrying them out. This means completing work with deadlines well in advance, so you have plenty of time to check over the task and make sure everything's up to standard.

3. Be productive but not busy. Deciding on what's most important to do should reduce the amount of time you are spending juggling tasks that keep you busy, and streamline your productivity. There's nothing worse than having a day where you are so busy that nothing gets done properly, if at all. Ranking the tasks and completing them in order of importance should reduce this panicky feeling of being busy all the time, and instead allow you to be as productive as possible within the given time-frame.

4. Handle any time wasters. There's nothing worse than trying to complete work and being distracted by something, especially if it's someone else that's distracting you. If your working environment is too loud, then try moving to a calmer more productive space, or if that's not possible, try putting in earphones. Other people's interruptions shouldn't be an excuse for you not completing your tasks. Let the people around you know what you need to do, and how you intend to do it, so that they won't bother you until you're done.

5. Rewards System. Telling someone to stop bothering you is easy when compared to stopping yourself from getting distracted by your own bad habits. This is where your will power really comes in to play. It's healthy to take a break from your work every few hours, but constantly checking social networks or making yourself a drink every half hour can be destructive to your work flow. Recognise what is useful to you and what's nonconstructive; if you don't need the internet for your task at hand then there's no need for you to use it.

How to Train Yourself in Time Awareness

As everyone knows, we all have a bio-clock inside. However, not all people can tell the time of day without a watch, or sing a song in correct rhythm. Here are 3 exercises that can help you within weeks.

Steps

1. Warm up! Pretend to be a pedal: Not literally swinging yourself. Try looking at a clock and count with it every second passed, say for 15 seconds. PATIENCE is the trick. You will get a better sense of how long is one second. Then back the volume and adjust your speed (usually you will sing too fast). Keep trying and you will get hold of rhythm.

2. What's the time: Every time you want to look at the watch, ask yourself to guess (or actually to feel) what time it is. Then look at the watch. Tell yourself how much ahead or behind you guessed, and the correct time. In 2 weeks, you can easily tell the time of day within 5 minutes difference.

How to Successfully Complete Projects

Your ultimate goal in rendering a project is to finish on time, below budget and with a happy client. But how do you perform it? Here are five tips to assist you.

Steps

1. Remember that the saying goes "Honesty is the Best Policy". You have to be honest all the time in dealing with your customers. Tell them if their project is not feasible or if you don't acquire all of the resource, cash and time involved to carry it successfully from the start. Set their anticipations by saying to them what you will carry and by when. And if it eventuates that you can't render on your promises, then state to them about it directly. By having an "open book" policy, you'll have your client's confidence. And if you involve them early enough, they will be a lot supportive to your cause.

2. Preparation is the key. You don't expect a successful presentation when you gone over it only twice. You have to prepare very well and make proper research.

3. Allow yourself to breathe. Always try to sit back and relax even when on a tight schedule. This will do you some good.

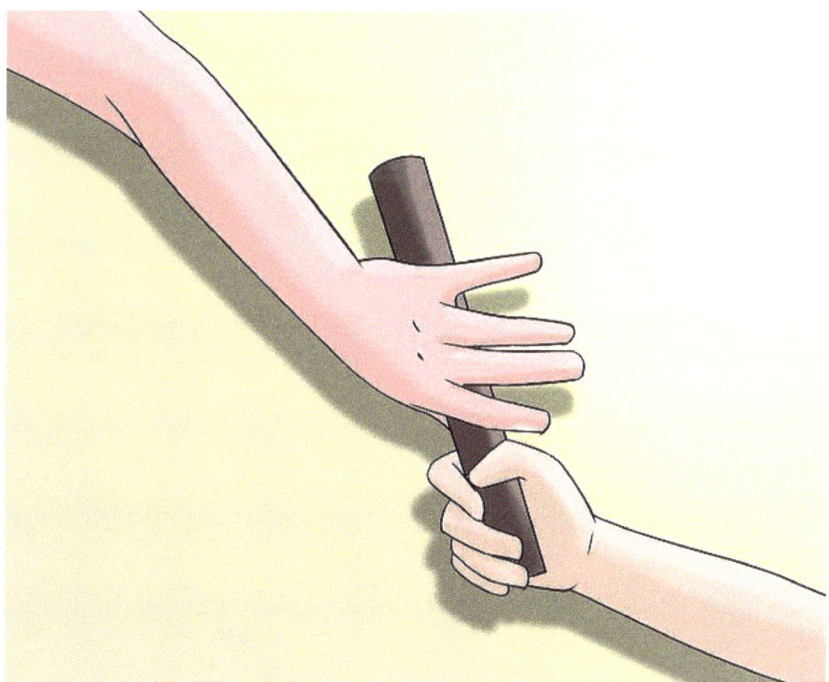

4. Hand it over. Managers oftentimes fall into the trap of believing that they can manage things much efficiently than staff. Of course in a lot of cases they may be right, but the problem is that they don't have the time to perform everything themselves. So a bright manager always tries to delegate as much as possible to staff. It presents them the time needed to supervise the project and support their team. It's a delicate task, but even if you recognize you can do a job more expeditiously than others, delegate it anyway.

5. Become a leader. When you economize time by delegating your jobs, you have more time for leading and motivating your group. Make this by regularly communicating the project to your team, honoring them for progress and accrediting their accomplishments. Have their respect by showing them you care. Build Up team liveliness by bringing them to lunch on a daily basis and uttering about what they accomplished unitedly. Remember, there is no "i" in "team".

How to Prioritize a Schedule for Optimal Time Management

Most of us feel like we have too much to do and not enough time to do it all. This combination often leaves you feeling overwhelmed and stressed. Learning how to prioritize a schedule for optimal time management can help you gain control of your life by focusing on what's important and getting it done.

Steps

1. Write down all of the appointments and tasks you want to accomplish in any given day or week.

- Lists are an important first step in prioritizing and time management.

- Prioritized schedules must allow time for family. When you ignore family, everyone's unhappy.

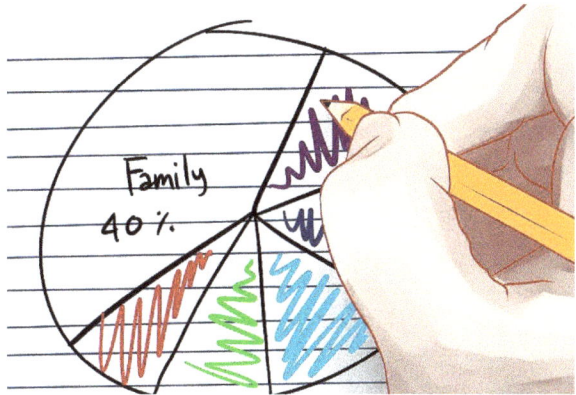

- Don't forget yourself. What's an important personal goal you want to accomplish this week?

2. Number or prioritize tasks in order of importance. A common time management tool often used to prioritize tasks and schedules is to:

- Give each activity that is important and urgent an A.

- Assign a B to important tasks that aren't urgent.

- Finally, place a C by anything you would like to do but doesn't carry any urgency or importance.

3. Choose what tasks can be removed from your list or that you can delegate to someone else. Then do it.

4. Note which quick tasks you can accomplish during wait times. Perhaps the time you spend on a mass transit commute or at your child's soccer practice can be used for tasks like checking email and voice mail, making phone calls or revising a report.

5. Check email once in the morning and once in the afternoon, and that's it. This is a popular time management tool used to deal with one of our biggest time wasters.

- When you stop what you're doing every time your computer chimes with a new email, you get off task.

6. Decide what needs to be completed first. A prioritized schedule means completing A tasks first. Completing your most important tasks contributes to a feeling of accomplishment.

- If you have a meeting with others scheduled first thing in the morning that you've decided is a B task, obviously it takes priority in your daily schedule, unless you can switch it for later in the day.

- Consider what time of the day is best for you in terms of thinking clearly and accomplishing more. For many, it's first thing in the morning, but you may be different. If you know that you're in the zone in the late afternoon, then make certain you're scheduling your A tasks for that time.

- C tasks should never be worked on during your high energy time. It's a waste of your resources.

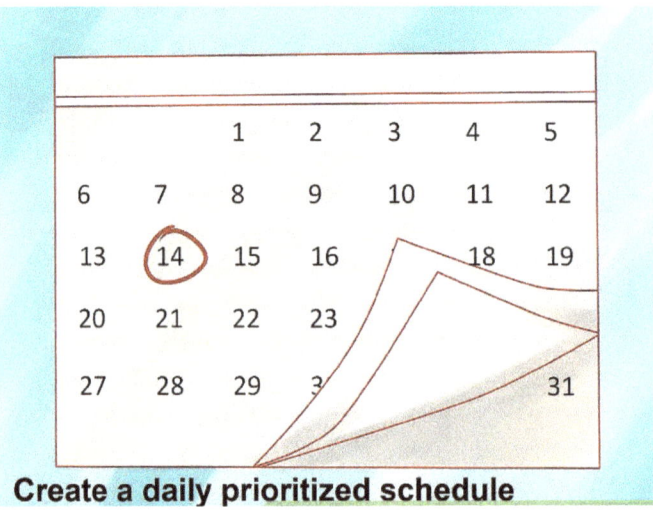

Create a daily prioritized schedule

7. Create a daily prioritized schedule from your list.

- Display your daily schedule where you will always see it.

8. Establish a reasonable goal of what your want to accomplish in a single day.

- While you may only want to concentrate on A tasks, these often take a lot of time. Instead, look at a mix, such as three As two Bs, and one C in a prioritized schedule.

- Say "no." No matter how full your daily schedule is or how well you prioritize tasks, some-one will ask more of you. Politely say no instead of feeling like this is the apple that will upset the apple cart.

- Chances are the person doing the asking will be surprised when you turn him down. You may feel a little guilty, but persevere.

- The more your turn down requests when you don't have the time, the more you send out the message that you're not a "yes" person.

- Sometimes you will want to say yes. If you have the time, fine; if not, look at your prioritized schedule and decide what you're willing to give up.

- Emergencies happen, but they occur far less often than we think they do.

How to Work More Efficiently with Time Management

You know your work flow is efficient when not only things are getting done, but you can shift your attention from one project to another with ease. This method will help you do that.

Steps

1. Know your what projects you need to work on. These are tasks that usually take an extended period of time to complete (over an hour); for instance, building your website, or developing a spreadsheet template.

2. Work on a single project for 1 hour 15 minutes

3. Shift your attention away from the last project or task and take a 15 minute break. You can do whatever you want that helps you move your mind onto something new. Doing something that moves your body helps.

4. Work another 1 hour 15 minute block. You can continue on the same project or move onto another one.

5. Take a 1 hour break. Reward yourself by doing things that are enjoyable and/or relaxing.

6. Repeat the two blocks of 1 hour 15 minutes of work with a 15 minute break in between.

7. Take another one hour break

8. Repeat the two blocks of 1 hour 15 minutes of work with a 15 minute break in between.

9. Enjoy the rest of your day.

How to Accomplish More in Less Time

We all have big dreams that shape our mind and future, but we don't always have time to fulfill them! Here is an article on how to achieve more in less time!

Steps

1. Start off by realizing your dream. This will help you in your future steps.

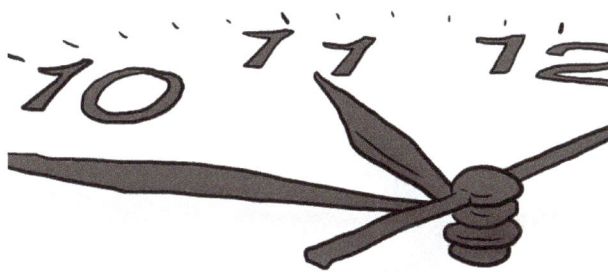

2. Make a timetable. Organising yourself will help you move through your work faster and you will have more time to spend on the little things that you love!

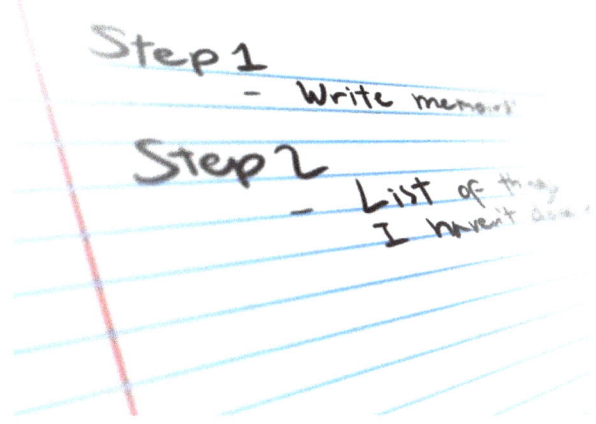

3. Make a list of steps. As good as it is to have a timetable, you need to know what you are doing!

4. Schedule breaks. As tempting as it may be, working over time hinders your progress.

5. Eat healthy and exercise! If you are working full-time, make sure to eat healthy and get plenty of sleep.

Mon	Tue	Wed	Thu	Fri	Sat
		1	2	3	4
6	7	8	9	10	11
13	14	15	16	17	18
20	21	22	23	24	25

Deadline!

6. Set deadlines to everything and make sure you follow them.

7. Award yourself! When you accomplish something on your list of steps, treat yourself to a night out or maybe even something as small as eating some chocolate.

8. Don't stop! The fire may be lit, but keep on adding more fuel to it. Don't let it die out.

How to Get Things Done Fast

Whether you're facing down a deadline or just trying not to waste too much time getting something done, a little extra attention and willpower will help you get through your tasks quicker than a speeding bullet!

Steps

1. Take a bit of time to plan ahead. Although planning may not be your highest priority, even a minute or two spent charting your course can help to get you there faster.

2. Keep a to-do list. Understand what you need to do. For certain sorts of tasks, you could keep this list in your head

- Don't panic or lose your head, even if the list seems long or daunting right now.

- Break down larger tasks into manageable parts.

3. Do anything you can to shorten the list. Is there anything you could delegate? Can you ask for help? Is there anything you can safely do later, perhaps after a deadline? Is there anything you could skip entirely? Are there shortcuts you could take or ways you could speed up the process? Can you ask for more time?

- Eliminate any time-wasters or low value activities or leave them on the bottom of the list until you have more time.

4. Recognize your priorities, and note them. This process can be as formal or as informal as you prefer, but you'll generally have certain tasks that are more important than others, and it's important that you focus on these tasks first.

- One way to consider priorities is to consider the impact of each task or sub-task and the consequence of not doing it or letting the deadline slip.

5. Take note of any deadlines you are working towards. If there are intermediate goals, give them intermediate deadlines, even if they are approximate.

6. Take note of your motivations. Try to state them as a positive (getting a good grade in a class, getting a problem solved) rather than negative (not losing a customer, getting in trouble). Your motivations will fuel your speed and extra effort and determination that you will need to get through the tasks.

7. Jump in and start. If it's hard to get started, do any little piece that gets you into the task. Generally, any start is better than no start, even if it's not ideal.

8. Work as quickly and efficiently as you can safely work. Balance your pace so that you are not working so quickly that you make mistakes that cost you further time.

9. Take breaks. As time allows, take short breaks to rest. For a project over many days, this means getting enough sleep that you can stay awake and concentrate. For a one-day project, a couple of minutes every hour will allow you to eat, drink enough water, use the bathroom, stretch (if your task is sedentary) or catch your breath (if it is physically active), etc.

- Don't take such long breaks that you lose your momentum. Rather than schedule them strictly, take breaks at natural stopping points in your work.

- Breaks can also provide a moment for intermediate planning or discussion if you are working as part of a group. It's a good idea to review your plan along the way and modify either your course or your plan, or both.

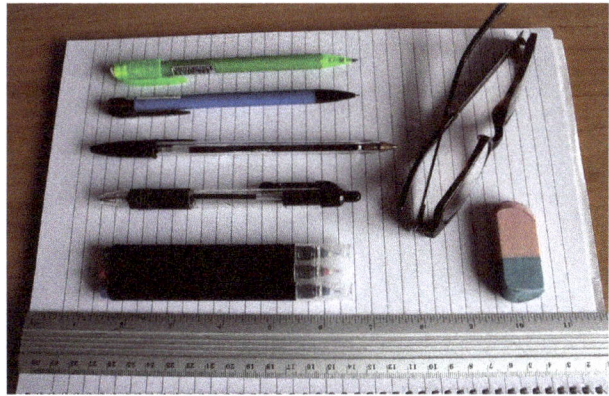

10. Be disciplined. Focus, be persistent, and be consistent. It will help to get through your tasks as efficiently as possible.

- If you find yourself losing focus, try to figure out why, and quickly. Are your objectives unclear? Do you need information from others? Are you getting stuck on something? Is your plan inconsistent with your progress or your goals?

11. Celebrate your accomplishments and get some rest as soon as you are done.

12. Do any required follow-up work. Let others know you have finished and give them whatever information they need to proceed with the next steps.

13. Take steps to avoid the next rush. Get ahead of your work

Different Methods of Time Management

Creating time schedules and planners are good ways to manage time effectively. Timetables help to focus on a task as well as relax and reinvigorate oneself when required. Planners help keep track of time and evaluate efficiency. This chapter discusses the methods of time management as well as provides key analysis to the subject matter.

How to Consider a Time Tracking Device

In a design, it is imperative that the project handler all together with the assistance of his team create and work out a plan schedule and timetable. Holding a plan schedule will supply an introduction on how far a project is anticipated to function before it can be rank and presented.

Steps

1. Create and work out a plan schedule and timetable. In a design, it is imperative that the project handler all together with the assistance of his team create and work out a plan schedule and timetable.

- Holding a plan schedule will supply an introduction on how far a project is anticipated to function before it can be rank and presented. This would also help in distinguishing the factors that may as a matter of fact hit the design's progress and estimate the number of time thought necessary to fulfill the job, the design's monetary budget, the survival of team members with the obligatory skill set and the assets essential to complete the design.

2. Know time supervision. It was stated that, once a project is well on its way, and a schedule is formulated, one of the superior obligations of a design director is time supervision. He should be efficient to track time on how long does a section or a person in his group requires to fulfill a special assignment. Tasks or responsibilities that are given to team members are usually straight or hierarchical. This symbolizes that the end of special job is the root of another.

- Every task is dependent with each other; therefore if single job is not accomplished in time, it would drive a delay of the starting of the subsequent obligation in the hierarchy. A domino impression will follow as the slowing of a task would pose prospective risks, extra costs and deficit of resources. It would likewise put some members of the group who are expecting the completion of the obligation before them to wait idly. Portion of programming should as well be the apportioning of time for contingency programmes in case a hazard beyond the design's control is experienced.

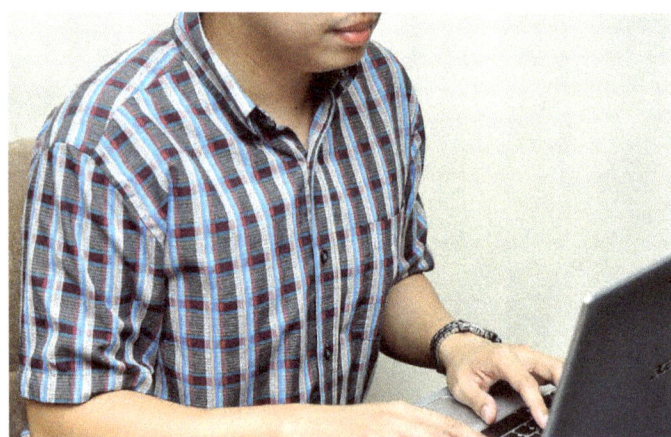

3. Monitor the growth. Time monitoring is really essential to the victory of the project as it will be of aid in lessening the possibilities of the domino outcome expressed above. If a project managing director is efficient to monitor the growth, he would be efficient to pinpoint what problems needs to be addressed and what can be set apart at a subsequent time. He would as well be provided with a bird's eye see of how the project is progressing, well discovering procedures that can be cleared upon on or moved out. He will likewise be efficient to look if his team is working in agreement to the schedule that they have organized.

- The practice of a time tracking software will as well assist in studying the project's weekly work flow, giving the plan handler a large breakdown of the schedule, correcting it each time the need arises. Web handling computer software is also a natural way to time track a plan. Carrying the data online would not only be advantageous to the design manager but it will also empower the team with the capability to monitor each other's progresses in a and schedule and simultaneously offering the customers with an up to date report.

How to use a Day Planner

You just got a new planner but have no idea what to put into it or fill out? These simple steps will help you fill out your planner and be organized.

Steps

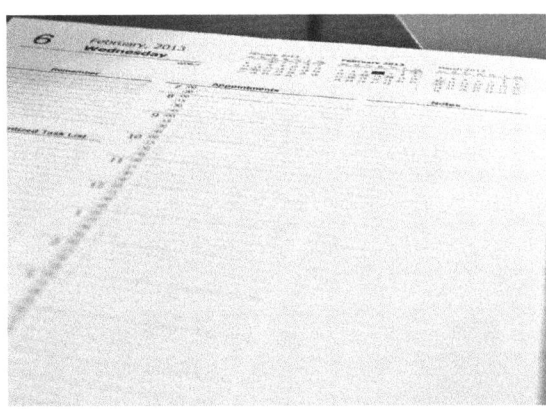

1. Get an agenda. It can be a weekly agenda or a day agenda. You might want to try out both and then decide which one suits you the most. In weekly agendas, you usually write down everything in a listing manner for your week. Daily agendas on the other hand, are used for listing everything day to day for more specific reasons.

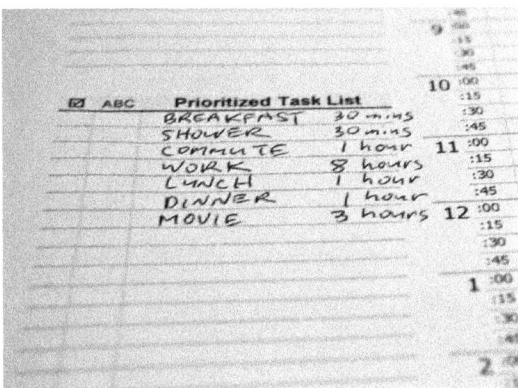

2. Think through about what you have to do each day and write it down. Beside the event you should put the time of the event. If possible you could try making the time 5 minutes earlier than the actual one so that you have 5 minutes to spare before it starts.

3. Next, add the times up to give you the time you should wake up at (you may use a calculator)

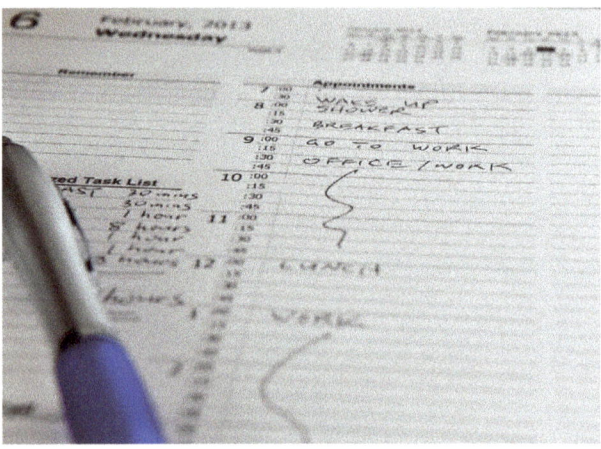

4. Write down the day plan in the notes page of your agenda/ write it down on the day you wish to try this out on.

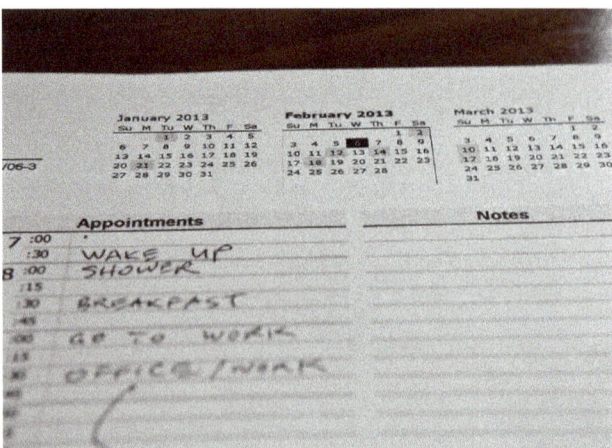

5. Try to do this weekly, planning ahead and writing down all evens for the week (for example do this on a sunday) will ensure you are not late to anything and do not forget certain events such as interviews, doctors appointments or classes .

How to Make a Time Managment Rota

Do you have problems with time? Are you always late? Well this article lets you in on the secrets of how other people you know can manage their time perfectly.

Steps

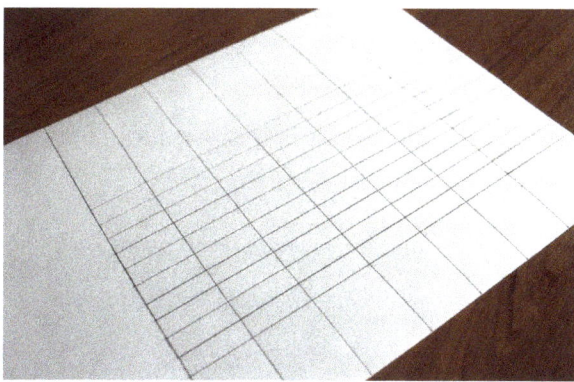

1. Get a blank sheet of paper and draw 7 lines going down and 12 lines going across.

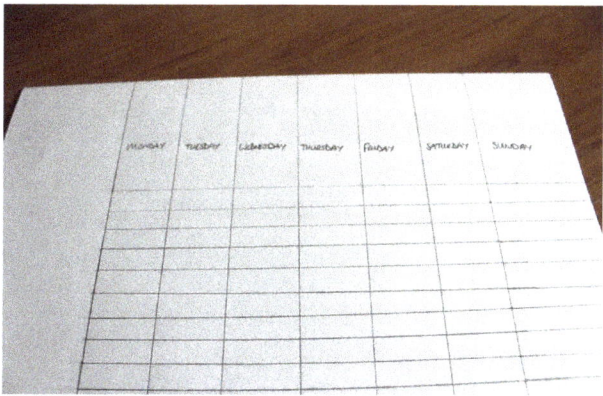

2. Name the seven boxes with the days of the week.

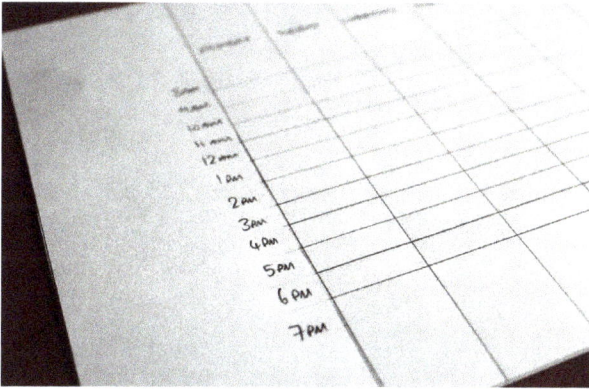

3. Name the twelve boxes for every hour.

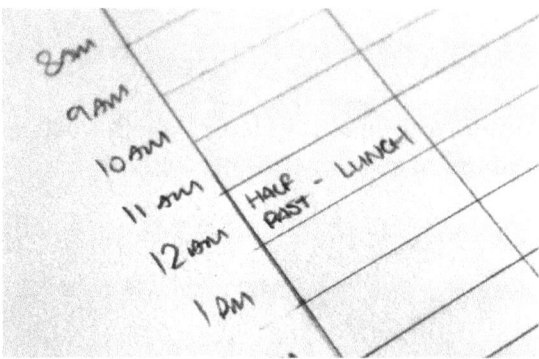

4. If you are doing something on that day and it is in the middle of 2 hours then write

How to Create a Time Management Schedule with Quadrants

Time management forms are one of the very important steps towards reaching your goals. Here is how you can manage your time effectively by making your time management matrix.

Steps

1. Draw a box with four quadrants.

2. Label the upper left quadrant as "urgent and important".

3. Label the upper right quadrant as "important but not urgent".

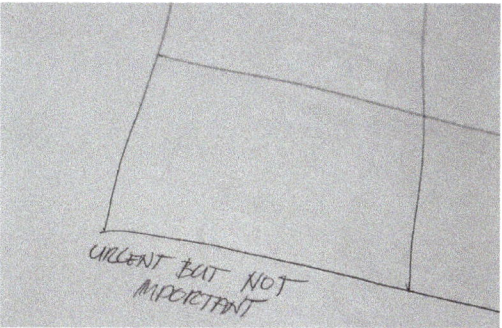

4. Label the lower left quadrant as "urgent but not important".

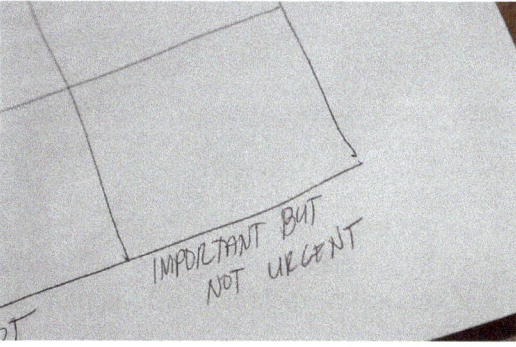

5. Label the lower right quadrant as "not urgent and not important".

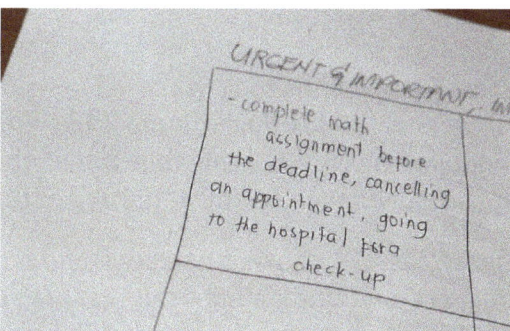

6. Classify your daily activities in the quadrants.

- "urgent and important" - e.g. completing math assignment before the deadline, canceling an appointment, going to the hospital for a check-up.

- "important but not urgent" - e.g. Preparation for the bi-monthly examinations, arranging an alumni meet, building relationships, personality development.

- "urgent but not important" - e.g. attending an unnecessary phone call, checking the junk mail, some interruptions.

- "not urgent and not important" - e.g. unnecessary chit-chat with friends, wasting time on the television, making unnecessary phone calls, video games.

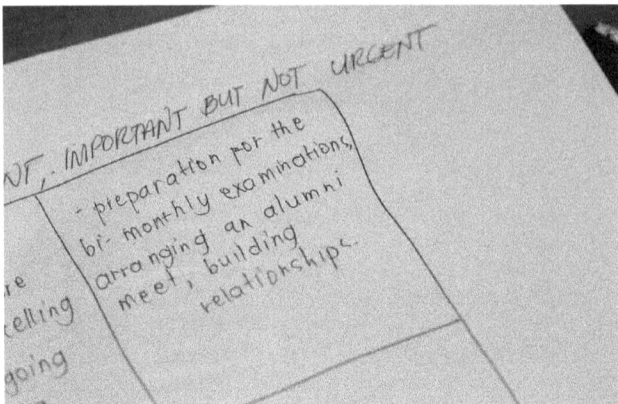

7. Aim to spend more of your time in the "important but not urgent" quadrant.

How to Track Working Time

Time is the only resource that cannot be stored for later, thus it's the most valuable. We can't afford to waste any minute. That's why it's essential for us to monitor how do we spend our time. It becomes even more important if you are a freelancer who is paid hourly. Then each minute has a very specific value- the value of your payout. Take a look at 4 simple tools that will help you to easily track your working time.

Steps

1. Use a watch, pencil, and paper. These are the tools you need to write down the time spent as you are working. The advantage to this method is that you don't have to use additional resources or technologies to record time spent. However, you waste time transcribing all those paper records to valid computer format so that you can do your billing at the end of the month.

2. Use a watch and a spreadsheet. Instead of using notebook and a pencil you can use computer software such as Excel, Open Office or some online solutions (e.g. Google Docs) to store information about your working times. It's advantageous as it's the least intrusive computer-based solution, helping you to prepare a working time report and costs calculation, but you waste time editing your spreadsheet.

3. Use a time tracking application. There are a ton of these on the market. All you have to do is to write a task name and press "Play" button. The single-purpose software is usually very easy to use; however, it requires you to have the computer handy to track time. You also need to add time entries and tasks manually.

4. Use Kanban Tool. Kanban Tool allows you to plan and organize your work (including assigning tasks to team members) using Kanban board and cards. You can track your working times with seamless time tracking module and analyze your results with time reports, which allows you to not waste time on adding tasks to your timers list, editing spreadsheet or preparing reports. It does, however, require you to have the computer handy to track time.

How to Make a Chore Chart

A chore chart is an excellent way to keep track of your daily responsibilities and maintain a well-kept home. An orderly home will make your guests feel more comfortable, your possessions last longer, and the overall atmosphere of your home more pleasant appearing and smelling. Add the fact that it's always easier to lay your hands on something put away in the right place, and it's hard to imagine why someone *wouldn't* make use of a chore chart. With a few supplies and an awareness of what needs to be done, you'll soon be checking off chores on your very own chore chart.

Part 1

Planning your Chore Chart

1. Write a list of all your chores. Take your pen and paper and take some time to think about all the chores that will need to be done to keep your home clean and orderly. Depending on your home, these chores may vary. For example, if you have pets of livestock, you'll need to include these in your chore list! Some common chores include:

- Cleaning the bathroom

- Dusting

- Making beds
- Sweeping
- Tidying bedrooms
- Vacuuming
- Washing dishes
  - Putting away dishes
- Washing laundry
  - Folding laundry

2. Choose the best schedule for your daily life. Take note of the schedules of those who will be doing the chore list. For example, if you're making a chore chart for your roommate who is generally busy in the morning but free in the evening, you chart his chore-work for evening hours.

- Chore charts can be as general or specific as you like. For those who have difficulty finding time to do chores, you may want a very specific chore chart and schedule.

- Some people find it easier to assign chores to a day, or even week. In this case, the person who has to do the chore will have an entire day or week to check off the chore from the chart.

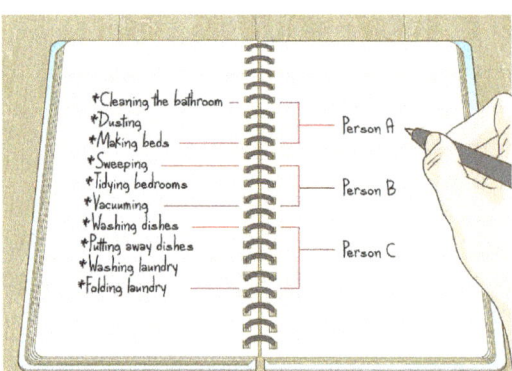

3. Divide and conquer. Not only will splitting up the chores you have make less work for everyone, it will also give a sense of solidarity to all involved. Even if you're a parent who doesn't need a chore

chart, listing your many chores next to the responsibilities of your kids might gain you more appreciation for all the work you do.

- This is a great technique for children who are resistant to chores. Once they see how much work you do next to their few around-the-house tasks, they'll likely be less difficult.

- Allow some flexibility with chore assignments. If someone particularly hates a specific chore, maybe a less hated one can be exchanged for it.

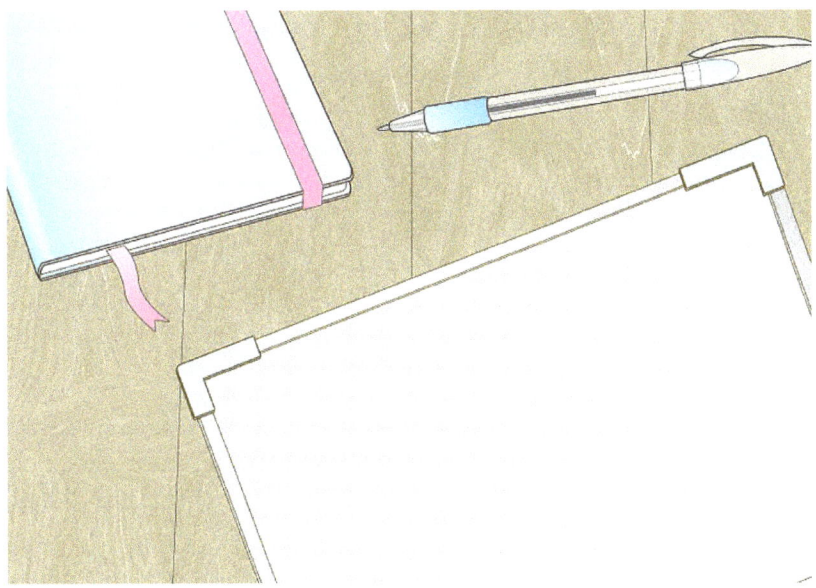

4. Gather your chore chart making materials. There are many different ways you can make a chore chart. You could even turn your chore chart into a personalized craft for your kids. Simply allow them to draw out their own chart on several pages in a notebook and decorate it with drawings, favorite characters, and stickers. Some other supplies you might find helpful include:

- Binder ring (optional)

- Card stock (optional)

- Dry erase board

- Dry erase markers

- Hole punch

- Notebook (optional)

- Paper (optional)

- Pen (optional)

- Stickers (optional)

Part 2

Making a Chore Chart

1. Prepare your supplies. Depending on the style of chore chart you're making, these may vary, but having all your supplies on hand will help speed you through your chore chart creation. For the purposes of offering a guided example, the following chore chart uses a dry erase board and markers.

2. Create a calendar with eight columns. The first column will be where you write down chore names, so you'll need it to be wider than the rest. The seven columns to the right will be where the chore-doer marks whether the chore has been finished or not. These seven columns can be much smaller than your first.

- If you have five chores, you should have at least six rows. The topmost row will be for days of the week, so you'll need one more row than your number of chores.

3. Draw a diagonal line in the upper left hand box. Do so from the upper left of the box to its lower right corner. In the bottom left triangle, write "Chores" to indicate the left column is for chores. In the upper right triangle, write "Days" to indicate the top row is for days. This way there won't be any confusion, and your chart will look tidy and complete.

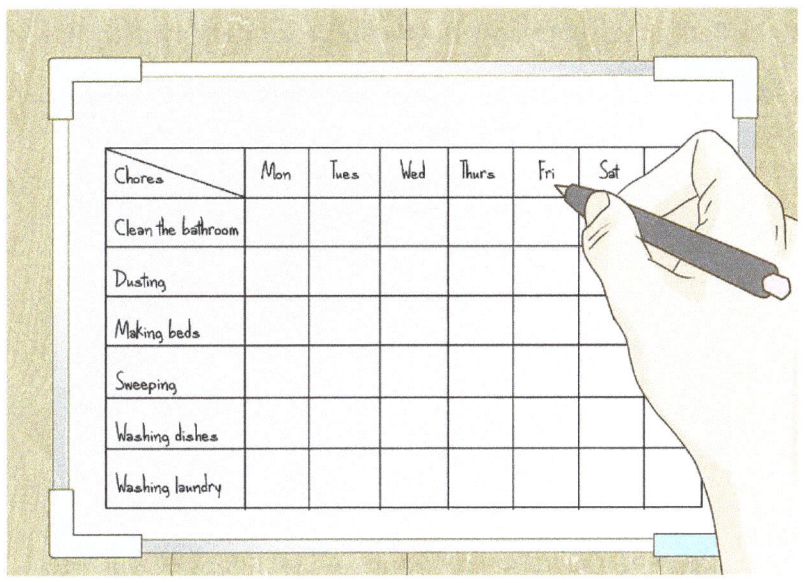

4. List responsibilities and write out the days of the week. Skipping the upper left hand box, write out the chores in the leftmost column of your chart. You might also want to include special information here. For example, for bi-weekly chores you might put "Bi-weekly" in parentheses below the listed chore. In the topmost row, skipping again the upper leftmost box, write the days of the week.

- If you don't have enough room in your top row to write out the entire name of each day of the week, use simple abbreviations, like: M, T, W, TH, F, S, SU

5. Mark off completed chores. This can be as simple as marking a chore complete with a check mark in the appropriate column when it's done. However, if you want to do the marking yourself to keep the chore doer honest, you can use the same procedure when you are informed the chore is complete.

- For example, when the chore doer's bed is made, you'll put a check mark in the box to the right of "Make Bed" in the corresponding column for the day of the week.

- For children especially resistant to chores, you may want to do a brief inspecting of the work before you hand out a check mark.

6. Offer chore incentives to make joyful workers. Even a small prize can be great motivation for a young child, but incentives work well for adults, too. If you have a roommate who's particularly messy, you can offer to buy him a pizza if he manages to stay on top of his chores for the month. Kids can be given small rewards, like stickers or small toys.

7. Use different colored markers for multiple people. Take your marker and write a color code at the top of the chart. For example, orange might be for Billy and green for Susan. Then, when each child completes a chore, you can write a check mark in the appropriate color.

- For chores that alternate doers per day, week, or a similar situation, you might want to use initials to mark the chore complete and keep track of order.

- For example, if Billy takes out the trash Tuesday but Susan is expected to on Thursday, initials would clearly indicate both whose turn it is and chore completion.

8. Separate chore lists for picky chore doers. Some kids, and even some adults, don't like their things to get mixed with others. This may be due to the greater clarity of having one's own chart, but regardless, you can satisfy picky chore doers by giving each person their own chart.

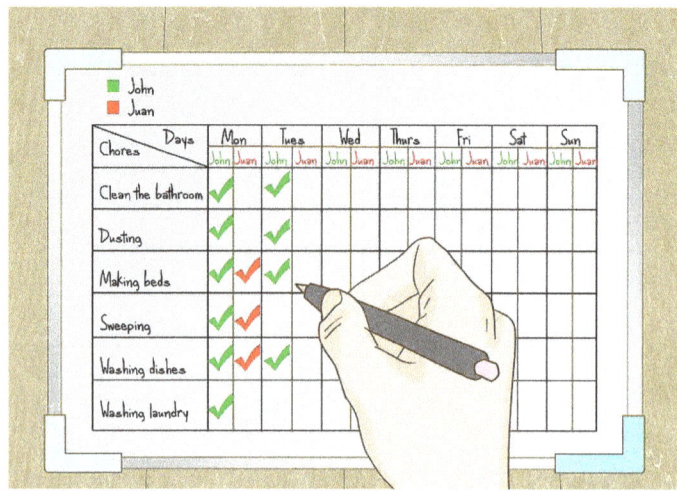

9. Make a daily and weekly chart with names in the columns. By making a daily chart, the chore doers will know that sometime during the day, all chores on the list will be done. This way, it doesn't matter which day of the week it is, all that matters is whether or not the chore was finished. Simply replace the days of the week with the names of the chore doers. When a chore is complete, it should be marked on the chart.

Part 3

Ensuring the Job gets Done

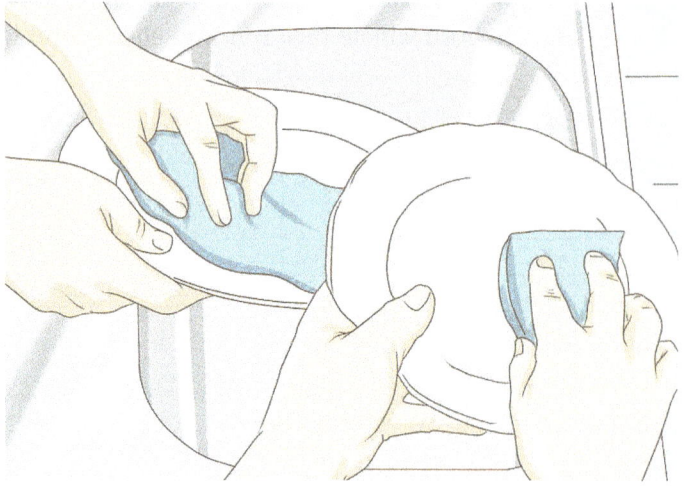

1. Supervise and lend a helping hand. If you are trying to teach your kids responsibility, you might not want to do their chores for them. However, by lending a helping hand or offering encouragement and advice, you can turn chores into a bonding experience.

- Play the word chain game while you work. Choose a category, and take turns while doing chores chaining together the last letter of a word in that category with the first letter of the next word. For example: *Category*: Sports

  baseball → luge → eight ball → limbo …

2. Offer reward for full completion. Rewards will be unique to each situation. Younger children can be persuaded to work diligently with small prizes, like stickers or dollar store toys. Older chore doers might enjoy a free pizza or a night at the movies. Whatever the case, a little motivation goes a long way.

3. Award points for chores completed. You can award more or less points depending on the difficulty of the task, but be sure you are consistent with your scoring. Unfairness can lead to stubborn chore doers becoming more resistant to your efforts due to a perceived lack of fairness.

4. Create chore reminder cards. You might notice that the chore doers consistently forget to clean something completely, or that certain aspects of the chore are avoided. In this case, you can improve accountability and squash excuses by writing out chore "recipe" cards. Simply:

- Write down all parts involved in doing the chore on card stock and punch a hole in its upper left hand corner.

- Put a binder ring in the punched corner.

- Leave the card in the room where the chore will be done.

- Attach the binder ring somewhere obvious, but out of the way. Maybe on the arm of a lamp, or onto a rung of a chair that sits off in the corner.

- For rooms that have multiple chores, you can collect several cards on the same binder ring.

How to Decide on a System for Time Management

Is your schedule a mess? Can't find time to hang with the kids? Are your friends mad because you keep blowing them off? Here's how to manage your time and keep track of your busy life.

Steps

1. First, calculate how many hours you have in a day (wake-up to bedtime).

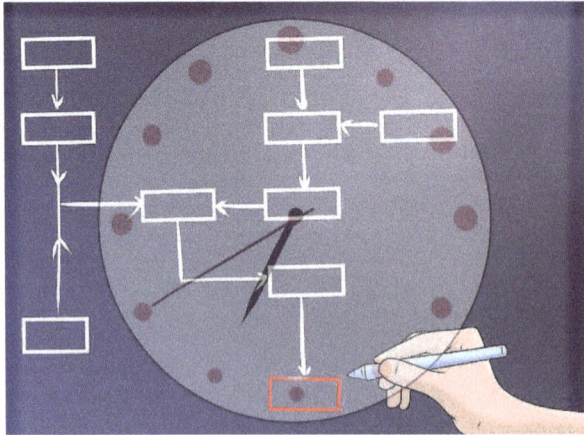

2. Make a chart. Divide each hour you are awake into halves. (30 min. increments) Write in the time frames as such (example):8pm (next line) 8:30pm....be sure to leave space in between lines for events and meetings and such.

3. Fill out every business meeting or work-related event first.

4. When you have finished with your business events, move on to personal events. If you plan something with your friends, make sure you find a time that works for you AND everyone else. This can sometimes be a hassle, but it is most likely worth a little trouble. Remember, you will need to plan time for transportation and things like that. If you plan something at 6pm and it takes half an hour to get there, plan to start driving at 5:30pm and be sure to write it down.

5. If you have kids or a family you need to spend time with on a regular basis, set a day or so and a specific time frame for each week, month, or time period of your choice.

6. When you schedule things for doctors' appointments or things like that, ask what days and times they have open. Make sure that time is available on your chart.

7. You can also set reminders for yourself if you have something you do a lot or everyday. Ex: Pick up kids at day care.

How to Avoid Common Time Management Mistakes

Time management is key for productivity and effectiveness. If you find that you keep making the same time management mistakes, you'll need to take concrete steps to turn that around. Luckily, it can be done with some hard work and concentration.

Method 1

Setting Priorities to Keep on Track

1. Make a "to do" list before taking action. You may want to just start working, thinking that making a list will slow you down. However, lists are key for most people when they have a lot to get done. Make a list and create a system to know what each item's level of priority is. Some people use a "A – F" system similar to a school grading system. Choose a system that will work for you.

- Your system may want to include the amount of time you think each task will take. For example, if one item will take half an hour but another will take several months, there should be a way to notate that on the list. Break down the big, long-term tasks into steps and make lists for the coming days/weeks.

2. Stick to high priority items first. Don't get off-track by doing easy things first, or things that are more appealing first. There is a difference between importance and urgency. Most people who are great at time management are able to make this distinction and act accordingly. When you do things based on a sense of urgency, you allow your time to be controlled by the needs of others rather than by your own needs. Instead, assess how important a given task is, based on your personal goals.

- Remember that the carelessness of others does not constitute an emergency on your part. They will need to learn to stay on top of their own responsibilities.

- Urgency is sometimes used as an excuse to put off doing something that's more important but also more difficult.

- If you see yourself prioritizing something unimportant, ask yourself if the current task is bringing you closer to your actual goal and vision.

3. Avoid taking on too much yourself. Don't get bogged down by trying to do every single thing yourself. Find aspects of a project or task that you can outsource or delegate to coworkers or employees whom you trust. The more you delegate, the more time you'll have for other things.

- Delegate tasks that can easily be done without your involvement. Think about what your skills and gifts are and how they're best used. For example, can you send someone else out to pick up the copies while you do the skilled work of editing the presentation?

- If you have a hard time letting go, create systems so that you can maintain oversight. For example, make sure you're cc'ed on emails or have a weekly meeting to check in on work that was done in your absence.

4. Avoid saying "yes" when you shouldn't. It's great to challenge yourself and to take on things that feel like healthy stretches. However, many people say yes to things when they don't actually have the capacity to complete them to the best of their ability. Learn to say no when you need to.

- Also, if able, learn to say no to things you don't like. Being passionate about your responsibilities makes you more likely to get them done, and done on time and well.

- Setting boundaries is important because it shows others that you can't simply become their safety net when they've taken on too much themselves.

- If you fail to set boundaries, others will likely keep piling work onto you, which will make keeping on top of time management even more difficult.

Method 2

Keeping Track of Time

1. Try not to lose track of time. A very common mistake is losing track of time. Your time is valuable. You want to know where it goes so that you can spend it more wisely. Once you know the ways that your time is spent, you may be surprised to see what you can afford to cut from your day and how much extra time you can make for yourself.

- Keep a large clock visible, unless this causes you significant anxiety. Visual prompts can be very effective. Also, are you more likely to look at and respond to a digital or analog clock?

- You can use your computer or phone to "clock in" and "clock out" of certain tasks.

- Write down the hours and minutes that you spend on a given task. This alone is likely to improve your focus and time management because you'll be aware that you're being timed.

2. Learn how much time things take. Many people repeatedly fail to plan by not knowing how much time things take. Tracking your time is a great way to learn how much time tasks actually

take. You can also look back on past projects and consider whether or not you had enough time to complete things based on the amount of time you'd set aside in the past.

- People who are considered overachievers are especially likely to underestimate how much time things take.

- Always budget in time for breaks. They are key to staying fresh and effective.

- Always remember to account for travel time! A lot of people calculate from the time they need to be somewhere, not the time they need to *leave* for somewhere.

- Budget in extra time as a contingency. What if the supplier can't deliver a rush order? What if a team member is sick and someone has to pick up the slack?

3. Avoid multitasking. The results are in: multitasking doesn't work. Unfortunately, humans are really designed to focus on and complete one task at a time. Don't think that you're going to save time by doing multiple things at once.

- Multitasking will most likely lead to a lack of focus and poor performance all around.

- Do not leave your email open or your cell phone out. Alerts from these will derail you. Focus on the task at hand and set aside another time to respond to emails, texts, etc. Set up a system for emergencies that need to get through to you.

- If you have a hard time not multitasking, repeat the mantra, "Right now, I'm focusing on____."

Method 3

Staying Goal Oriented

1. Set goals. Many people start out with a goal, but lose track of their goal sometime in the process. This is a common time management mistake. Having strong personal goals is essential to managing your time well. Goals give you a destination to work toward and help you keep track of your vision. If something isn't directly in line with your goal, it's a distraction.

- You can have goals for the hour, the day, the week, the month, or the year.

- Use visual prompts. Have a place where you post that day's goal and see it frequently to help keep you on track throughout the day.

- Write down long term goals, too. These can be goals of where you'd like to be in five or ten years. Check in periodically to see if what you're doing is helping drive you toward those goals.

2. Don't lose sight of the big picture. The big picture is the larger set of visions and goals. It will help you keep perspective so that you don't get bogged down in details or distractions.

- Sometimes perfectionism is important and sometimes it's not. Look at the big picture to help you determine whether "good enough" is alright for a given task or whether you should be focusing on minutia at any given moment.

- Check in with others if you see yourself losing perspective.

3. Avoid distractions. Get rid of clutter around your desk or workplace. Cleanup your computer's desktop. Do what you can to create a focused, harmonious workplace. This may mean turning off your phone or email alerts during designated work times.

- Don't check personal email or social media sites when you're working.

- Throw garbage away immediately, shred old documents when they're no longer used, and file past projects out of sight.

- Turn off music or other background sounds to help you stay focused.

How to Organize your Schedule

Make time every day for work, for play, for loved ones, and for time alone. To do this, you will need to organize your information in a way that makes sense for your lifestyle. Make or purchase a planner that makes sense for your scheduling needs. Make a prioritized schedule so that you can pace your daily and weekly tasks.

Part 1

Getting a Planner

1. Buy a paper planner. Visit your local bookstore or go online to purchase a planner. You can purchase a paper planner that spans one or more years. Pick an attractive planner, so that looking at

your schedule is a pleasure. Pick a small or flat planner that will fit in your bag, so you can carry it with you.

- If you would rather not carry a planner with you, consider a desk planner that will sit comfortably on a table.

- Make sure your planner has enough space in it for you to write down your daily activities.

- If you have a variable schedule with lots of small parts, get a planner with large spaces per day.

- If you have many ongoing projects with flexible deadlines, pick a planner with small spaces per day but plenty of extra blank page space per week, so you can keep a to-do list.

- A to-do list that is part of your planner is useful to most people, so consider a planner with facing blank pages for every week.

2. Plan online. If you coordinate your schedule with others, or if you do most things on your phone and computer, it might make more sense for you to pick an application, a website, or an extension of your email services to organize your schedule. You can look up free mobile and web applications that suit your needs. If you plan on sharing information from your online planner with friends, family, or colleagues, ask them what service they use and plan accordingly.

3. Plan on your computer. Most computers come with a calendar application. You can coordinate this application with your email and other websites you use. Search your computer for "calendar," or scroll through your applications folder.

4. Make your own paper planner. You can find printable templates online, or you can design your own planner by hand or on your computer. Purchase a case for your planner, such as a three ring binder or a book cover. If you are printing templates and putting them in a binder, use a hole punch on your templates and put them in your binder.

- If you are binding your own book, try taking the pages out of an old hardcover book. Lay the cover flat and measure it.

- Find paper that is slightly smaller than the length and width of your flat cover, or cut paper to size.

- Fold each individual page in half to make two pages of your book.

- Using a ruler and pen, colored pencil, marker, or paintbrush, draw lines on each page according to the organizer design you prefer. Look at templates online for ideas.

- Stack your pages. Make sure they fit in your cover. You may need to create three distinct stacks for your book to lie flat.

- With your pages now in order, put in dates. Don't forget holidays!

- Bind your book. Take an awl or large needle. Punch one or two holes in the cover in the same place. Use a sturdy thread to sew together.

Part 2

Managing your Time

1. Keep a prioritized schedule. Avoid keeping a long list of tasks that keeps getting longer. Instead, integrate your to-do list into your daily schedule. When you learn of a new task, break it into parts

and write each part down under the date that you will do it. Make sure you note its deadline, in case you don't get to it on time.

- You might want to keep a schedule of daily tasks and a to-do list of running projects, but consider keeping a weekly to-do and a monthly to-do instead of one long list.

- Keeping a list of unscheduled tasks leads will cause you to burn out on your projects before you even do them.

2. Start with the biggest tasks. Start your day by tackling the most important item on your agenda. Schedule the first order of business to be the one thing you absolutely must accomplish that day. That way, if you are interrupted later, you will have at least done the most important thing. Anything that is due or is especially important is a good candidate for a first task.

3. Break every task down. Schedule every part of each task, including emails you have to send, planning you have to do, and items you need to get. Otherwise you might waste time sitting down to accomplish something only to realize you are missing essential ingredients.

4. Consider before you act. Before you start each task, spend a few minutes thinking about what you want your end result to be. This will help you be more directed and focused. Write your goals for each day or each task down in your planner, or simply sit and think. If you are working with someone, state your goals aloud.

5. Break your days into blocks. Devote each block to one task. Multitasking is less efficient as a rule. Focus on one project, even if that project has diverse parts, during each block.

6. Give yourself time off. Scheduling time off sounds counterintuitive, but it will help. Do not plan on overworking yourself. Working through exhaustion and bodily needs should only happen in

emergencies. Schedule short breaks every 45 minutes to an hour, as this is as long as most people can focus.

- Take time away from your desk or computer.

- Schedule time with loved ones, time to prepare meals, and time to be alone.

- If you are prone to anxiety, try scheduling "worry time." That way, if you find yourself spinning into worry while you are trying to work, you can put it aside for later.

- Schedule downtime and leave your distractions to that time. Instead of constantly checking your phone, your email, and social media, do it during scheduled blocks.

How to Make a Timesheet

As a small business owner, you can elect to have your employees complete time sheets rather than punch a time clock, or you may want your employees to track how much time they time spend working on different projects. Rather than use standard forms that aren't specific to your business, you can create your own time sheet using a word processor and spreadsheet program.

Steps

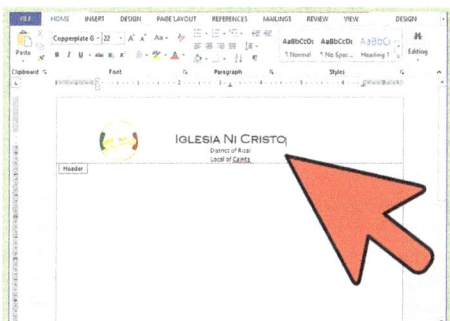

1. Create a document in your word processor. Put the name of your business at the top and add your business's logo if you have the file available.

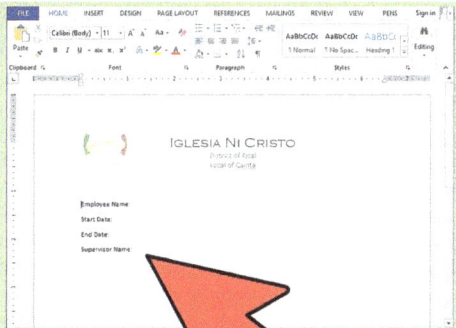

2. Add lines for your employees to enter their names, the dates the time sheet covers and other information, such as their supervisors' name.

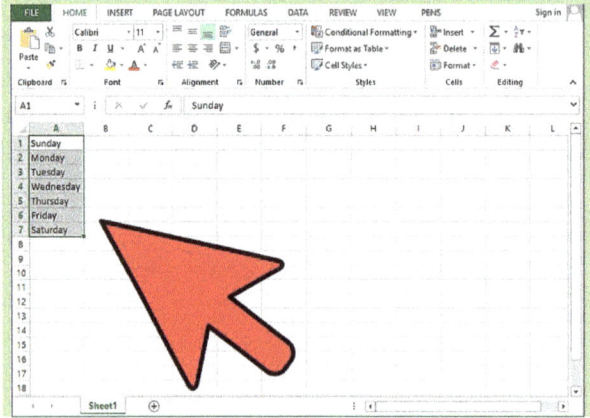

3. Open your spreadsheet program. Some word processors allow you to open a spreadsheet within the document and will provide the appropriate menus for you to create and format the worksheet.

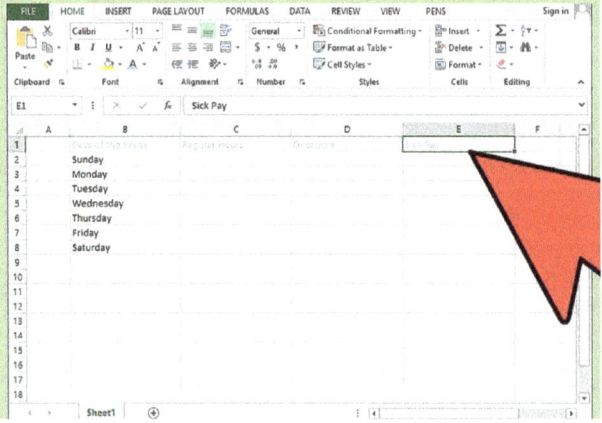

4. Along the left side of the spreadsheet, enter the days of the week.

5. Label the top of each column for the categories of work you pay your employees for. For instance, you can enter regular hours, overtime hours, sick and vacation pay. Label the last column for the total number of hours worked per day. You can also create separate columns to record hours of work completed on specific projects or for specific clients.

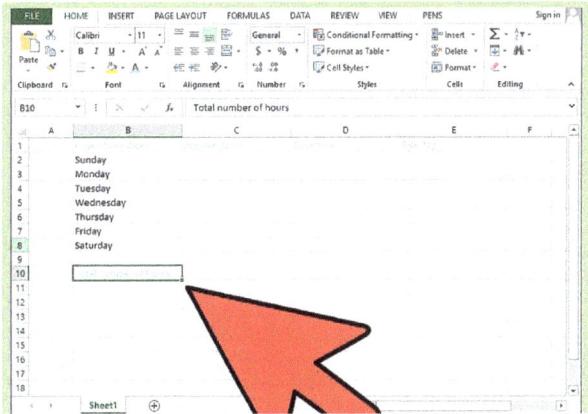

6. Designate a row at the bottom of the spreadsheet for the total number of hours worked in each category.

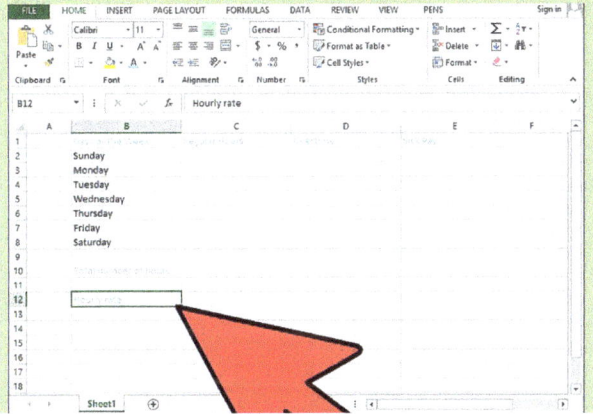

7. Add a row, if you prefer, for an employee to enter her hourly rate for regular hours, leave and overtime. If compensation is confidential and someone other than the bookkeeper and the employee's supervisor will see the time sheet, leave this row off or instruct your employees not to fill in this row.

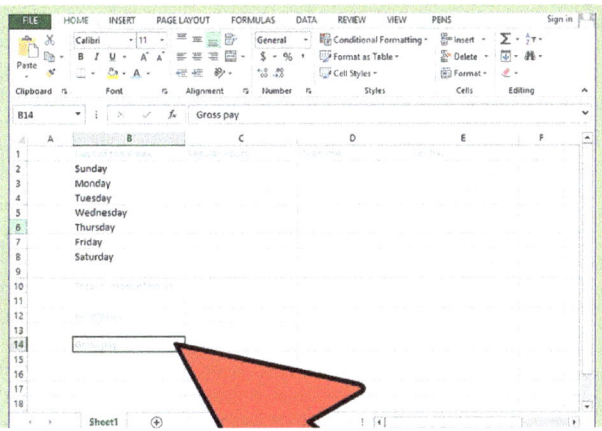

8. Finish with a row for total hours multiplied by the pay rate for each category of work and a cell for the week's grand total, which will be the employee's gross pay.

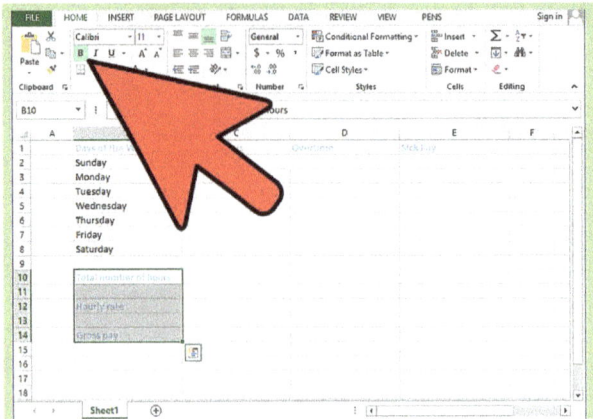

9. Improve the look of the spreadsheet by using bold print for the labels and shading in the label rows with color.

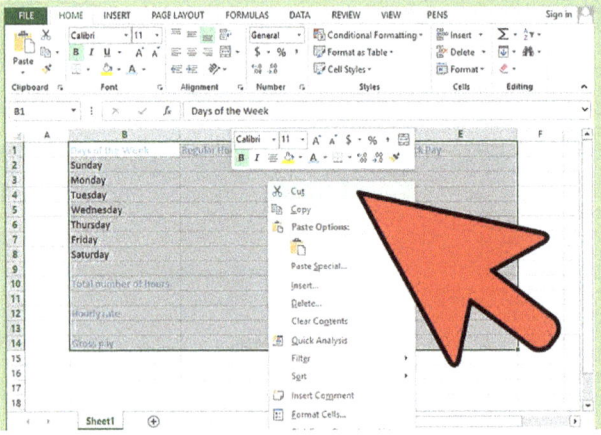

10. Cut and paste the spreadsheet into your word processor document. Most software bundles allow you to send the spreadsheet to the other document and will trim and size the spreadsheet to fit. If not, you must adjust the size of the rows and columns to make the spreadsheet fit.

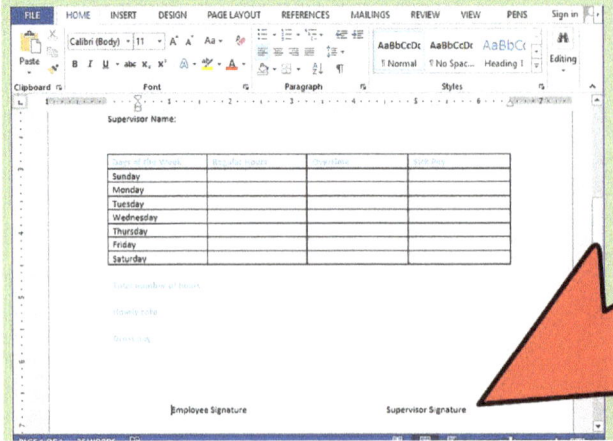

11. Include lines below the spreadsheet for the employee and supervisor to sign, verifying that the hours listed are accurate.

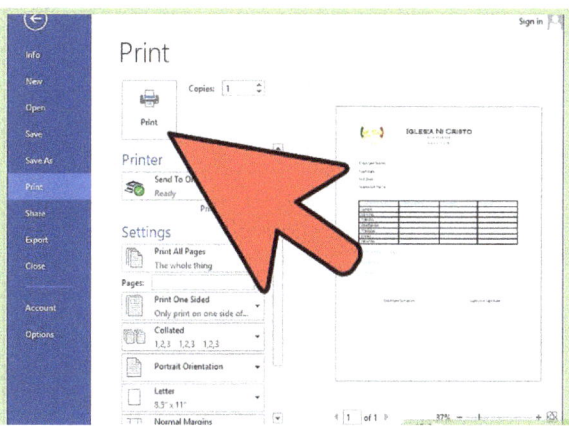

12. Save and print the document, make copies and hand them out to your employees. It may be helpful to use a yellow highlighter to write "ORIGINAL" across the master copy so employees won't use it, forcing you to print out another copy.

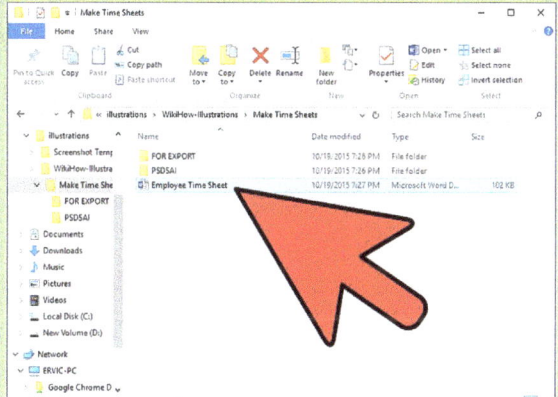

13. Invite your employees to keep their time sheets on the computer by making a copy of the file available on your network server. Be sure to protect the original file so your employees cannot use or corrupt it.

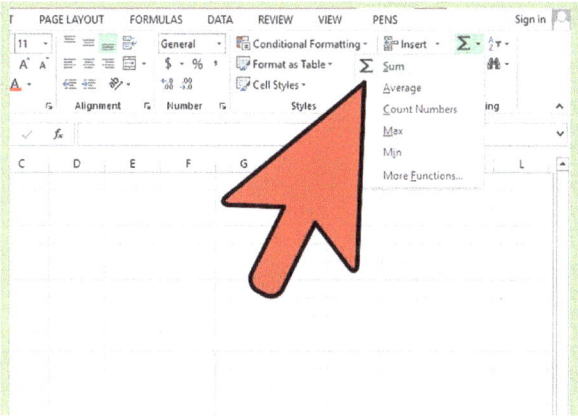

14. Use the spreadsheet's quicksum or autosum feature to have the program add up the number of hours in each row and column and enter the result in the total row and column.

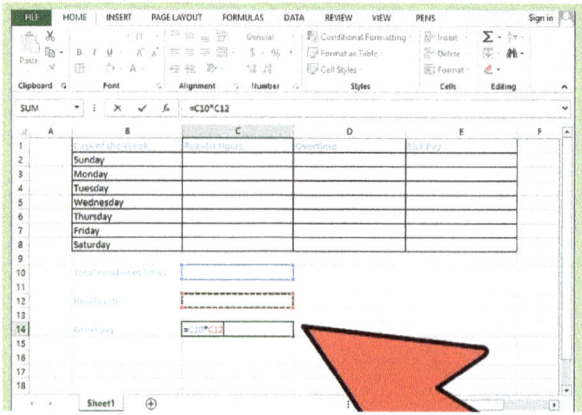

15. Create a formula or function to multiply the total hours for each category of work by its pay rate, and use the quicksum and autosum feature to determine the grand total for the week.

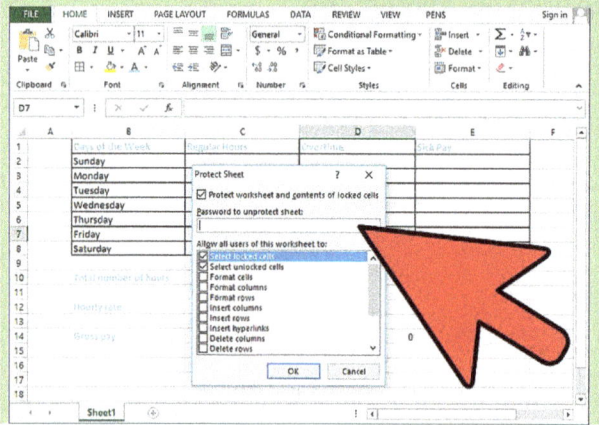

16. Find the spreadsheet feature that allows you protect your time sheet's labels and formulas from being edited or erased. Specify that these cells cannot be altered, but that your employees can fill out other cells.

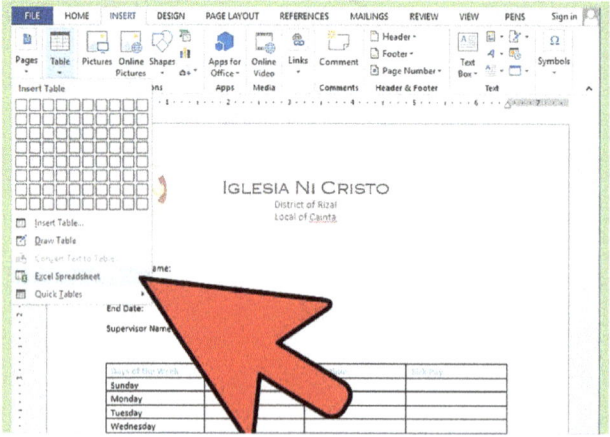

17. Insert the spreadsheet into the word processor document and test it to make sure that it will recalculate automatically after an employees fill it out.

How to Customize a To Do List by using Templates

Organization is important both at home and in the office. In fact, the better your organization, the better your productivity will be each day. It is important to manage your time and your tasks carefully each day so you can increase your productivity and be more professional. While this may seem like a second job, using a template can greatly speed up the process and make it much simpler. In this article, you will learn how to find the best template for your to do list needs and how to use these templates to organize your life both at work and at home.

Part 1

Finding a template list

1. Find the template that meets your to do list needs. Search online for sites that provide free to do list templates suitable for Microsoft Word.

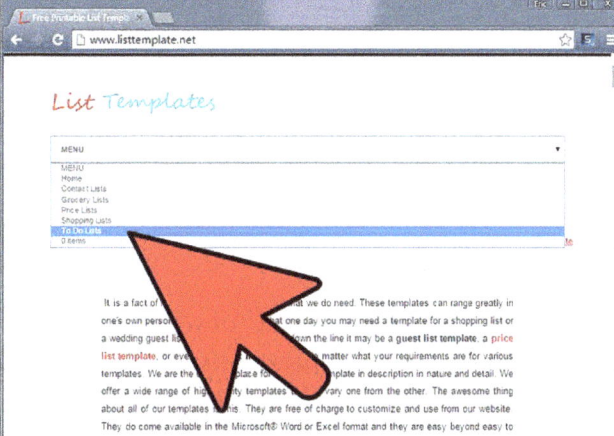

2. When you arrive at the site you've chosen, click on the category for the type of list template you are looking for. Browse through all of the templates available. For example, if you need a to do list, click on the to do list templates.

- Alternatively, use the search bar of the site to navigate the to do list templates.

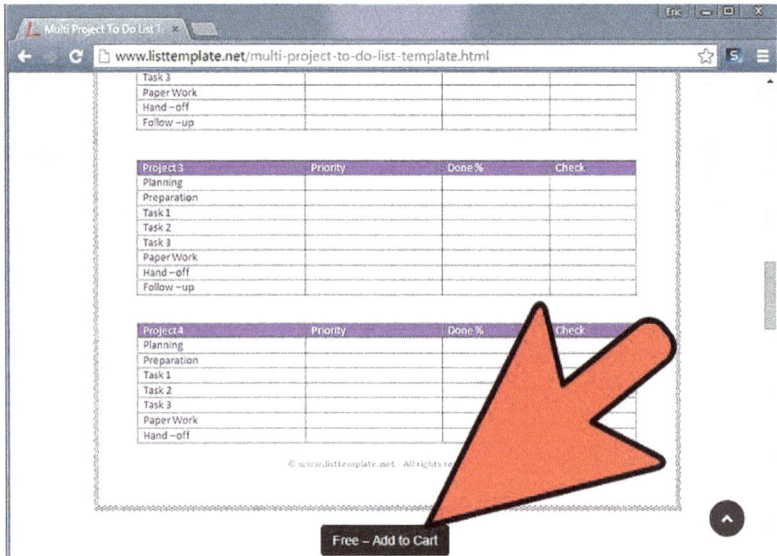

3. Once you have navigated to the list template section you need, browse through the available templates and select the one you need. For example, if you are looking for a "project to do list" template, click on that template and download the template by clicking the "Download, "Download Template" or "Free - Add to Cart" button after the template preview.

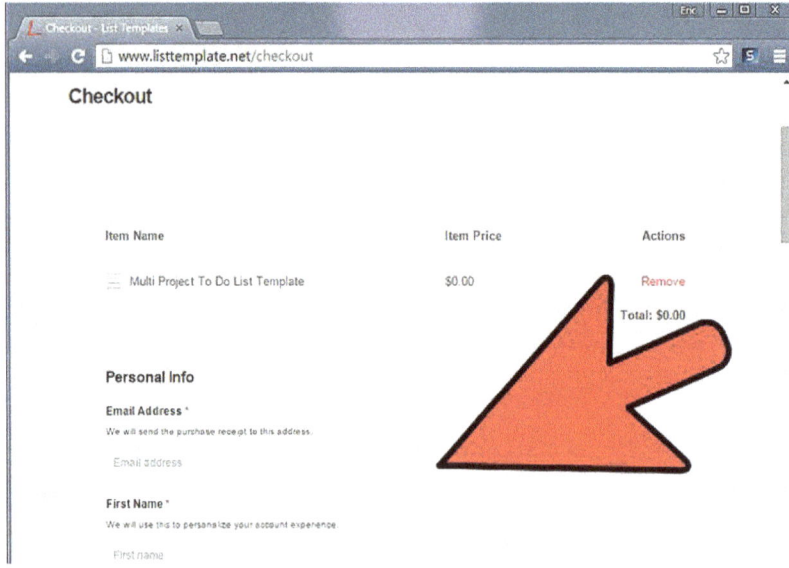

4. When you have selected all the templates you wish to download, click the Checkout Button. From the checkout page, you must enter some basic information such as email, first and last name for security purposes and you must agree to the site's terms and conditions. You will not be charged anything for the templates as all of the templates are made available completely free.

- If you are using Official site of Microsoft or vertex42 there is no need fill the form you'll be direct to the template after clicking on download button.

Part 2

Using the List Templates site

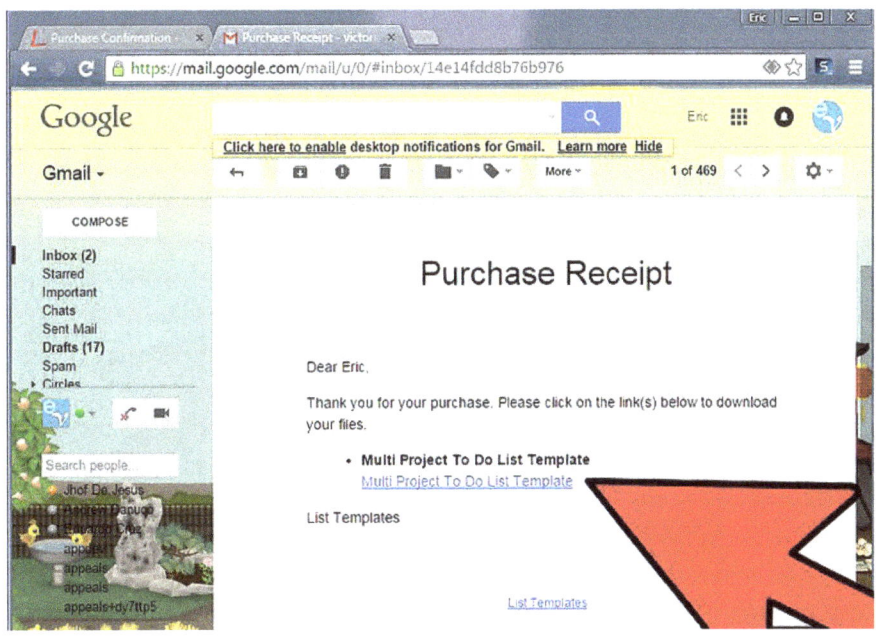

1. If you use the List Templates site mentioned earlier, expect to receive an email. After you complete the checkout process, you will receive an email with the download instructions for the template(s) you have chosen. Click the link provided to start the download.

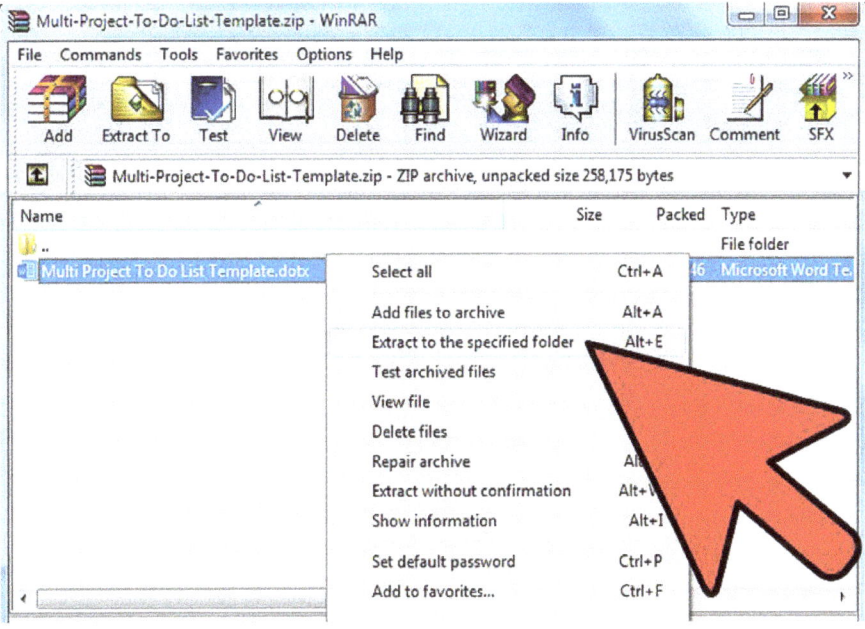

2. Unzip the file. The file downloaded to your computer will be a zip file. Double click on this file to extract it and open it in your version of Microsoft Word or Excel. While any version will work, the latest version is the preferred version to use with the template.

Part 3

Customizing template to do lists

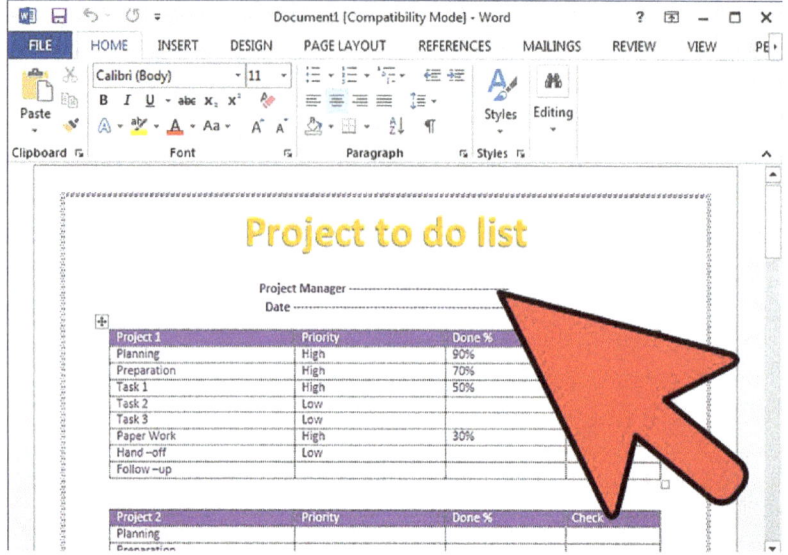

1. Now that the template is open on your computer, begin to edit its various features to customize it to your needs. First, edit the header section of the template and add any information related to your tasks and add any logos you wish to use. Simply change the placeholder text such as "Company Name" with your company in order to customize it for your specific needs or business.

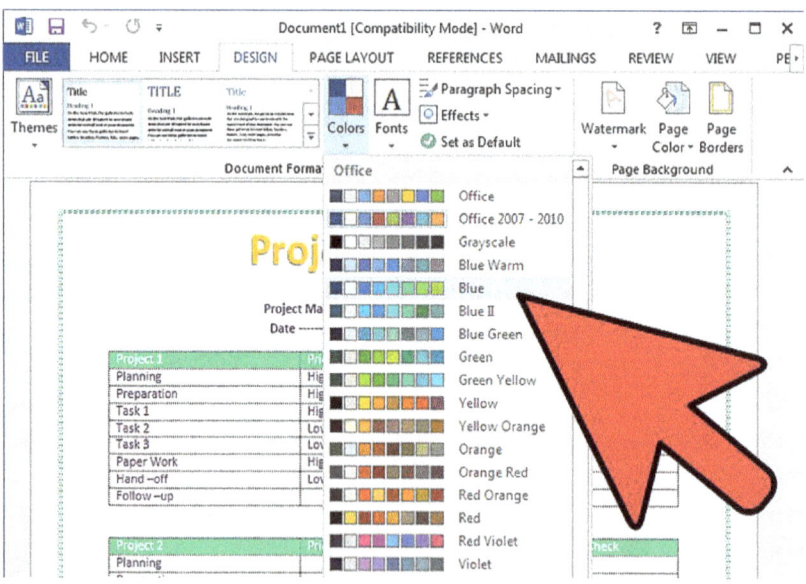

2. While the template has probably already been customized with colors and other font settings so it looks professional and interesting, you may want to make a few changes to the template to truly make it yours. Simply navigate to Page Layout > Colors and Themes to make the changes that you want.

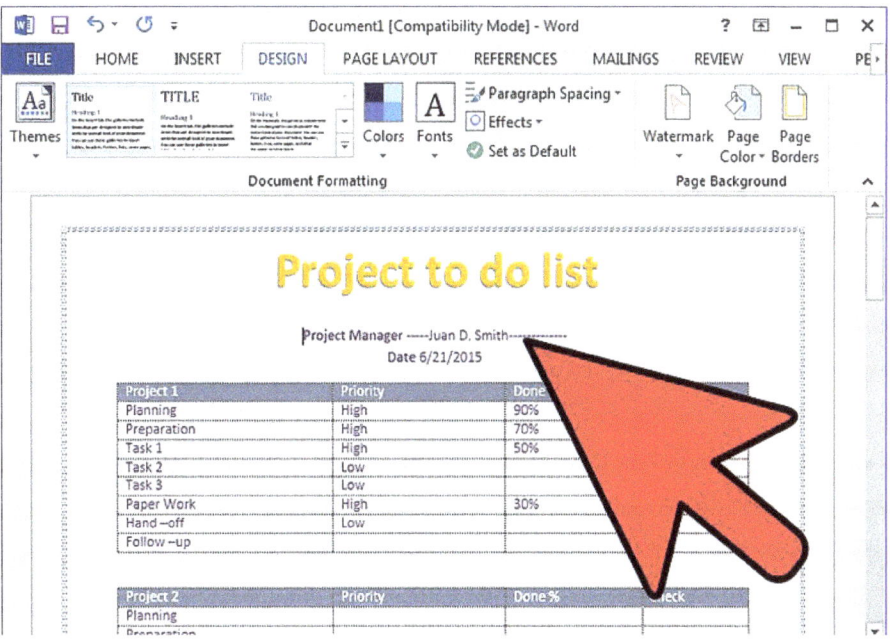

3. Double check that all your changes and customizations are correct and that they look good on your screen. Once you have double checked everything, you can now begin adding the tasks you need to complete into your template.

Part 4

Finalizing and using your customized to do List

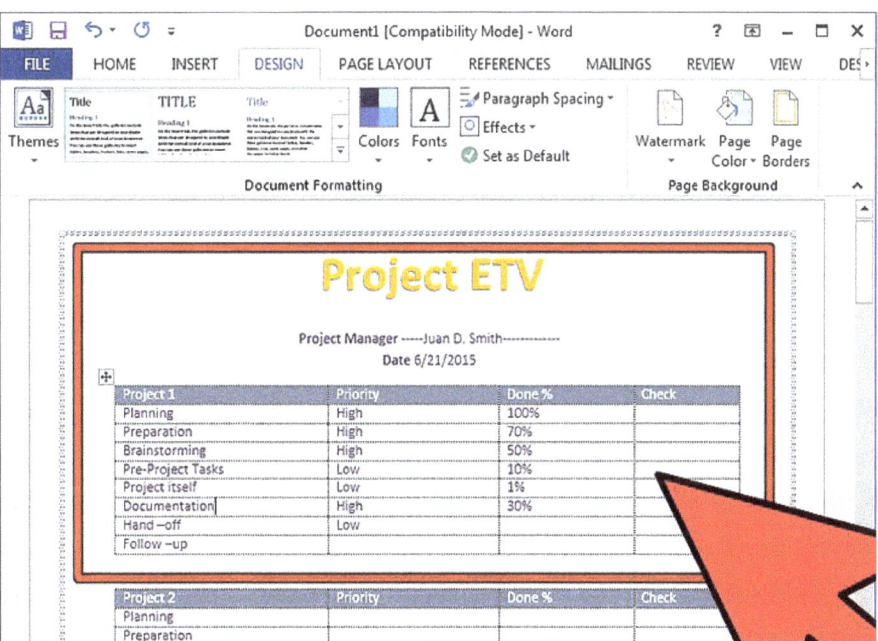

1. Proofread all the details and tasks you have entered to be sure everything is correct. Once you have checked the list you are free to print it or share it with others.

2. Remember that the key to staying organized is to continue to utilize these to do lists each and every day after you create them. By doing so you will be able to increase your productivity while never forgetting to do something noted on the list. This will be sure to impress your coworkers and superiors and might even help you to advance your career as well as reducing your stress levels, egardless of how busy you may get.

How to Stop Wasting Time

Are you always staring out the window for countless minutes, even though you have work to do? Do you research useless information or play games on the Internet when you know you have more important, pressing tasks? It might be time to admit that you have a tendency to procrastinate. The key to managing your time more effectively is to minimize distractions, focus on the most important tasks you need to complete, and to find a reliable way of gauging your productivity.

Method 1

Avoiding Time-Wasting Habits

1. Stay off the Internet. With the Internet rarely more than a click or tap away, it's no wonder that we constantly battle the urge to check our various bookmarked sites. When you know you need to stop wasting time and work on something, avoiding the Internet is an easy way to avoid procrastinating.

- If your willpower alone can't keep you off the Internet—or worse if the work you need to get done involves using the Internet anyway—you can install site-blocking tools for various browsers. Simply turn on the application when you need to keep focused and let the program be your willpower for you.

2. Keep your email inbox closed. A survey of Microsoft employees showed that they spend an average of ten minutes responding to an email, and then a subsequent fifteen minutes refocusing on the tasks at hand. If you really need to focus on a specific task, set an auto reply on your email and refrain from checking it until you've finished the work.

- The same basic principle works for text messages, instant messages, push notifications, mobile alerts, etc. These distractions help us procrastinate because they often feel more productive than other time wasters, but they rarely are. Turn off your phone completely when you can if the separation anxiety from the connection won't serve as its own distraction.

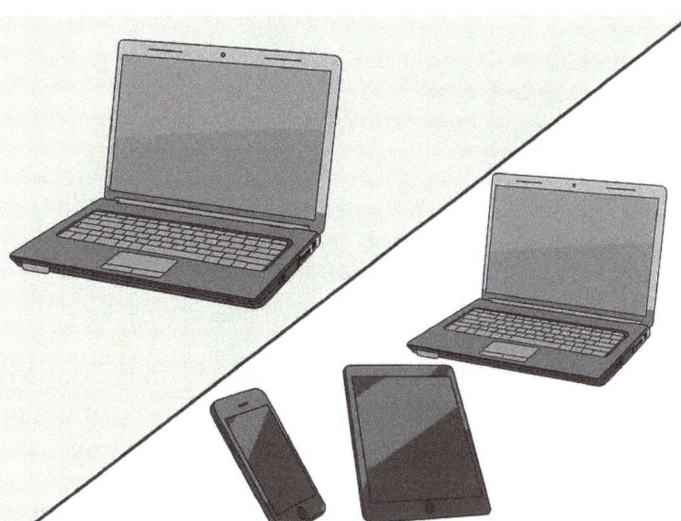

3. Do all of your work on one device. Switching between a laptop to work on a spreadsheet, your phone to check an email, and a tablet to pull up a presentation is a recipe for disaster. Each time you move between devices, you likely succumb to a distraction or two, and then have to refocus

yourself. As often as possible, try to collect everything you'll need on one device during a prep period before you get started, so you can work from one device as you go.

4. Write out a schedule. Most people hate the idea of keeping a complete calendar, but not all scheduling has to be this complete. When you set out to complete a specific task, take five minutes to make a list, outline, or applicable timetable for the task. By giving yourself a manageable timeframe, you're also more likely to hold yourself to the work at hand.

- Using "time boxing," or fixed time segments for specific tasks also breaks them down into more manageable pieces, making the wide open workday feel easier to engage with. This practice can work with everything from homework assignments to office jobs to home repairs.

5. Go slower. Sounds utterly counterproductive to time management, but trying to work too quickly or multitask on anything more than menial tasks can end up wasting time. Studies have shown that only 2% of people can multitask in truly effective, time saving ways.

- Going slower also gives you the opportunity to ensure that you complete each task fully and clearly, making it less likely that you have to go back and clarify or fix mistakes, which can end up taking more time.

6. Stick to the task at hand. It's no secret that many college students have sparkling apartments in the week before finals. We often procrastinate by taking on other important (albeit non-time sensitive) tasks instead of the most important task we need to complete. Spending time on less important activities is still a step backward and a time waster when you have other deadlines or due dates looming. Recognize when the task you're working on isn't the one that should be at the top of your list.

7. Give yourself a stop time. Working without a stop time in mind is a sure way to burn yourself out and get frustrated. Whether your stop time is the end of the workday, when you have a dinner scheduled, or something entirely different, having a finish time in mind will help stop you from overworking yourself, which will only lead to a decline in the quality of the work regardless.

- Even if you're in crunch mode with a term paper due the next day, schedule breaks that give you enough time to collect before getting back to it.

Method 2

Using the Repeat Test

1. Create a form to manage your time for the day. Now that you have a collection of steps to help you stay focused from Method 1, the repeat test is a great way to test how effectively you use them. Start by creating a spreadsheet or even simply drawing a form on a piece of paper or a whiteboard. Make one column with the hours in your day listed, and then make a wider column leaving space to the right of each hour.

2. Stop what you're doing at the top of each hour. This test requires you to take a minute or two at the top of each hour to evaluate how you used the preceding hour. Set a timer if you need to ensure that you stop long enough to fill in the form.

3. Consider how you spent the hour. During your evaluation period, consider what you completed over the previous hour. This can be anything from an exercise routine to studying for a test to spending the hour in front of the television. Be honest with yourself regarding how you spent the hour.

4. Ask yourself if you'd repeat the hour. This is the step from which the test draws its name. Once you've taken stock of the hour, simply ask yourself if you'd repeat it. The question essentially seeks to make you ask yourself if you believe you spent the hour in a productive manner. You're less likely to repeat the hour if the answer is no.

5. Summarize the hour and write down your evaluation in the righthand column. Keeping a written record of the day to see how many hours you would repeat and how many you wouldn't is also an effective motivational tool. Write a few words about what you did with the hour in the righthand column and as well as your repeatability evaluation.

6. Acknowledge the parts of your day over which you have control. One of the drawbacks to the repeat test is that you can quickly fall into the habit of judging every hour by its overall utility. A class where the instructor doesn't cover new material, an unproductive work meeting, and other parts of your day can start feeling like frustrating time wasters in themselves. Try to remember that you don't have complete control over every hour of your day sometimes and that meeting an obligation—such as being present for the unproductive meeting—can still count as a necessary portion of your day.

3   Time Management in Daily Activities

In certain professions, time management is a fundamental requirement. Leading a team or a project requires planning and computation of potential time that would be needed to finish a task. Multi-tasking and preparing a to-do list are basic ways to tackle effective management of time. The major aspects related to daily time management are dealt with great details in the chapter. It provides a step-by-step account of achieving these routines as well.

How to Effectively use Time Management Skills

Time management has become very important in this competitive world with so many activities to do! It is important to manage time to do everything you like and also have some time for relaxation.

Method 1

RELAX

1. Take a book or paper to jot down your goals or plans.

- Sit back and relax. Put all the thoughts out of your mind. If possible, meditate.

- Set your mind free to make further plans.

2. Make sure all your goals are realistic. Unrealistic goals will only make you feel more stressed and WASTE your time.

- Write down your long term goals. Ex: " I want to become a model".

- Go through the list, one by one.

- Cancel those goals that are not realistic. Ex: Becoming a doctor might be just your childhood goal but you no longer want to become one or you might have written that only because your parents want you to become one. Cancel this because you are no longer interested in that profession.

- Now, you have PRIORITISED your goals.

3. You have now come a little closer to managing your time effectively.

Method 2

PLAN AND ORGANIZE

1. Once you are ready and clear with what you want to achieve and what you have to do to achieve, things are lot more easier.

- Now that you have your list of goals, plan he next step- "What do i have to do to achieve my goal?".

- Suppose your goal is to become a model, then you have to concentrate more on your diet, posture, etc.

- Write down the things or activities that are necessary to achieve the goal.

- Find out if there are any short term courses which will bring you closer to your goal.

2. Make sure you follow it. Remember you cannot achieve anything without hard work.

- ORGANIZE

- After all the planning, you now know what you exactly want to do and how much time you have.

- Concentrate on your goal. Do everything to achieve it.

- Do not deviate from your goal.

- Plan your day accordingly. Ex: If achieving your goal requires taking dance lessons, keep 2 hours for it. Nothing is more important than doing what you really want to do.

- Other things can wait. Suppose, talking to your partner for an hour is a routine, cut it down to 30 minutes, so that you have 30 minutes more to concentrate on your goal, your life.

Method 3

DO NOT PROCRASTINATE

1. Long term goals were taken as an example and are important because they keep you focused on your activities. You also stay healthy and happy when you do what you really like. No one can stop you from achieving what you want if YOU DONT STOP doing what you like.

- do not procrastinate. Act from today, NOW.

- Finish off with what is more important and necessary, then you have all the left over time to relax, enjoy the day without the guilt of not doing what was more necessary and important.

How to Manage your Time when Housecleaning

Housecleaning can be a very time-consuming process. In fact, it often seems like it never ends, as things begin collecting dirt and dust soon after you've cleaned them. To avoid stress and inefficient use of your time, it is helpful to learn how to manage your time when housecleaning. The guide below will provide some tips for getting your cleaning done in a quick, orderly fashion.

Steps

1. Make a list of all the cleaning tasks that your home requires. Managing your time well is a matter of scheduling well, and enumerating your cleaning tasks will help you build a schedule.

- Aim for comprehensiveness. Include both frequent and infrequent cleaning tasks on your list. For example, frequent tasks might include laundry, sweeping, and washing dishes. Less regular tasks might include cleaning windows, dusting air registers, and deep cleaning your appliances.

- Next to each task on your list, estimate how often it needs to be done. For example, you might decide that dishes need to be cleaned daily, vacuuming can be done every 3 days, and cleaning out the refrigerator can be done once a month.

2. Arrange your cleaning tasks using a calendar. After deciding on the frequency of your house-cleaning tasks, you can begin building your schedule. This is best done using a month-to-month calendar; you can also build your schedule on a weekly or even yearly basis if desired.

- Begin by marking down your prior commitments on the calendar. For example, if a particular work commitment will absorb most of your time on a certain day, you won't want to assign yourself a time-consuming housecleaning task.

- Next, mark down your most frequent cleaning tasks on the calendar. For example, if you've decided you need to vacuum every 3 or 4 days, you might mark "vacuuming" down on each Monday and Thursday. As you fill in your frequent tasks, make sure to spread them out evenly. You may want to group related tasks (such as vacuuming and sweeping) on the same day.

- Now fill in your less frequent tasks. Weekly, bi-weekly, and monthly tasks can be filled in after your more frequent tasks. Once you have completed the entire month's schedule, you can use it for each successive month. Minor changes may be required by your work schedule.

3. Assign each cleaning task to the person responsible for it. If the housecleaning in your home is handled by more than 1 person, make sure each person's responsibilities are indicated on the schedule. These responsibilities should also be worked around other time commitments.

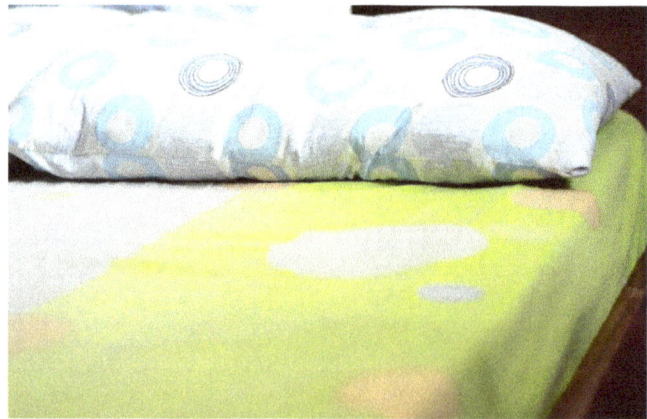

4. Augment your monthly schedule with a daily checklist if desired. You may find that there are some tasks that need to be done every day or on an "as needed" basis. You could consider arranging these tasks in a separate daily checklist. Examples might include making the bed and spot cleaning floors and surfaces.

5. Adjust your housecleaning schedule as needed. The entire point of the housecleaning schedule is to help you manage your time so that cleaning tasks don't pile up and feel oppressive. If the schedule itself starts to feel oppressive, don't be afraid to make adjustments. Shift responsibilities around or scale back the frequency of tasks until the schedule fits your needs and you are able to stick to it.

How to use Time Management in the Workplace

Do you know someone at work who can finish all the tasks assigned to them and still have time left over to pursue their hobbies, enjoy a lunch with their family and friends, go camping over the weekend and even take up more responsibility at the office? You do, don't you? If you think that colleague of yours has Hermione's Time Turner, you'd be wrong. There is no such thing as Time Turners or time machines (not yet). That dude or girl was able to do whatever he or she wanted because of proper time management. This article will show you how that's done.

Method 1

To- Do Lists

1. Accept the truth: one day means 24 hours. This applies to you and anyone else you may work with. Even your boss.

2. Get to work at least a half an hour earlier than usual everyday. Get a sheet of paper and sit down somewhere quiet. Take a deep breath and think about everything that needs to be done.

3. Prepare a list of to-do activities. First of all, draw a table with three columns- tasks, due date and priority. Make the column for the tasks the biggest.

4. Write down the tasks to finish, as they occur to you. Include the respective due date.

5. Prioritize the tasks and label them with 1, 2, 3 or A, B, C (high, medium, low priority):

- Tasks to be completed within a day or two would be high priority tasks. More time should be assigned to these tasks and they should be dealt with first.

- Tasks to be finished within a 7- 10 days would be of medium priority.

- Tasks that have two or more weeks to finish would be low priority.

6. Once you have completed all the above steps, all you need to do now is get to work and start checking off items when you finish.

7. Any task that you do not finish on that day get carried forward to the next day and so on. Keeping to the to- do list could feel a bit difficult if you are not used to it but stick to it for a day and it will get easier.

Method 2

Urgent- Important Matrix

- This method was popularized by Stephen Covey, A. Roger and Rebecca R. Merrill through their book "First Things First".

1. Get a small notebook. Sit down someplace quiet and think about all that you have to finish.

2. Write down everything you have to finish. Label them "Important" or "Urgent" based on the following criterion.

- Important would be those tasks that have to be completed in order to achieve your goals.

- Urgent would be tasks that require immediate attention.

3. Decide how important an activity is and rate it on a scale from 1- 10; 10 being most important. Do not think about how urgent an activity is.

4. Draw a matrix as depicted in the picture and label the quadrants.

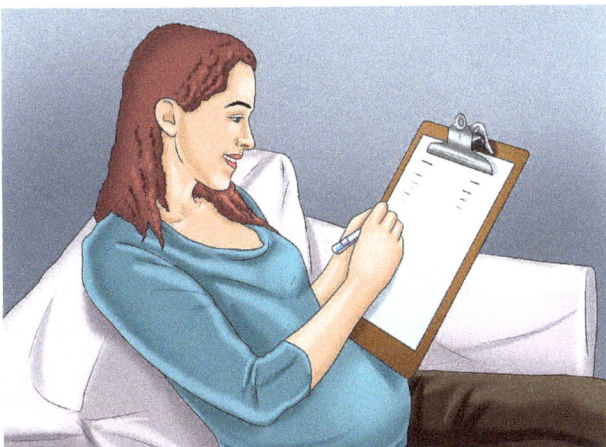

5. Write down your tasks into the quadrants according to the description below.

- Important Activities- These refer to activities that have bearing on your goals and is not urgent, that is, you have plenty of time to finish it. Example would be preparing a monthly report on your performance.

- Critical Activities- These refer to tasks that are important as well as urgent. E.g.: preparing a minutes of meeting or preparing a daily report on performance.

- Distractions- These are tasks that are neither important nor urgent and should be avoided if possible. E.g.: watching movie, chatting with friends etc.

- Interruptions- These activities are urgent but not important and the most common source of interruption would be your colleagues. E.g.: a quick 5 minute meeting with your boss, a colleague asking you for clarification on some document etc. If possible, these activities could be rescheduled to when it's convenient for you.

6. Check off the items as and when you complete them. Do not put anything aside for later. If you can do something now; do it.

7. When you are done with all the critical and important tasks; enjoy the distractions- listen to music, read a book or hang out with your colleagues at the watercooler.

How to Master the Skill of Time Management while Studying

How many people can actually say that they are expert at managing time? Well, I guess very few. This occurs same when it comes to study and revision. The great news is you can master to use your time productively and also reduce the time you have to spend in front of the books. Below are some steps that you can try to use your time wisely while studying.

Steps

1. Learn the difficult parts of revision and study first. Sure it will be easy to learn by studying the easiest parts first. However, if you leave the difficult parts for learning later, you may never understand it and the things may go in an opposite way.

2. Make plans. Make a plan and if you stick to your plan you will be just fine. Planning and preparation prevents from poor performance.

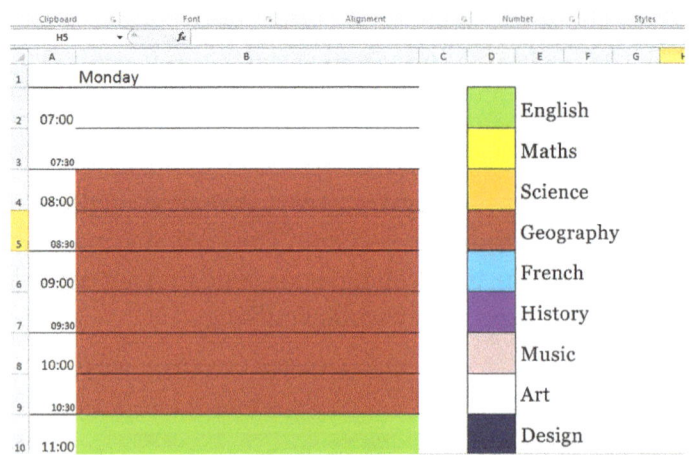

3. Make a timetable. You can make a time of the subject you wish to study each day. You can simply make written timetable or just can keep it in your mind.

4. Give importance to your time. Do not rush and do all the revision and studies in one go. Decide what needs to be done and determine in what order you are going to tackle it.

5. Avoid any type of disturbance. Unplug the internet, turn off your computer and mobile phone, and switch off your video game.

6. Set yourself objectives if you are going to work with others. If you do not set yourself with a goal then you may have a good time but you will achieve nothing.

7. Allocate your time carefully. If you are studying with a day job or with a family, you need to allocate your time carefully and cautiously. Your wife and children may want to spend time with you too. Also, your may want to check to works in the job.

8. Practice makes perfect. You need to practice to make sure that you can pass or get a good grade in exams.The less time you spend on one question the more time available to move to the next question, and also more chance to score a good grade. So take an alarm clock or a stopwatch and practice for your test using some model exam papers related to the exam.

Organizing your Time Wisely

Careful organization of tasks is important in short-term as well as long-term activities. Organizing and prioritizing tasks make them easier to accomplish. Effective time management helps to meet set deadlines and accomplish them. This chapter elucidates ways to organize time wisely.

How to Get Things Done on Time

Whatever you do from work to fun you need everything balanced and on time. This is how to stay on your schedule in a limited amount of time, something that can be hard to do.

Steps

1. Try making a to-do list or schedule to follow. If you have a plan of what to do you aren't forgetting things last minute. Keep a simple schedule, don't overdo it because this will make it hard to do everything in a limited amount of time and make you stressed. Organization will help you accomplish your goals.

2. Set the right amount of time and space in the day to finish each of the tasks on your list. Don't set too little time as it can make you stressed, and don't forget to set time aside for meals, sleep, family important things.

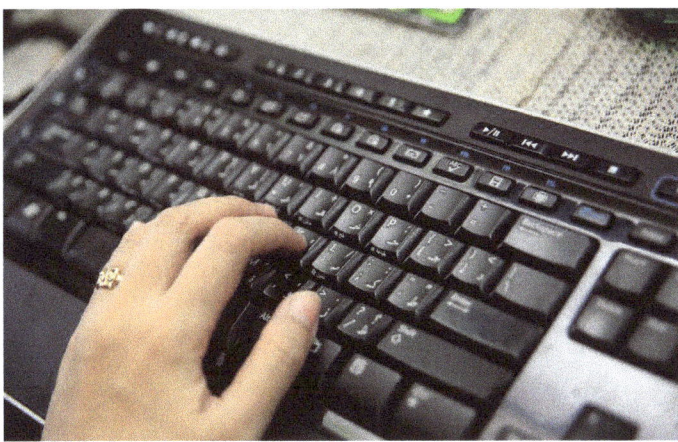

3. Stick to that schedule. If you don't stay to your schedule you won't have things done in the right amount of time. Like an exam paper.

4. Get some sleep. Without enough sleep our body can't function and do things in the time it could. If you get at least 8 hours a day and stick to that schedule too, you will be able to do things faster.

5. Don't procrastinate. Leaving things until last minute can throw you out of whack. And makes you stressed. Do the important things first then watch T.V.

How to be Organized

No one likes being disorganized. Organization takes time, but when you get the hang of it, life becomes much easier. To be truly organized, you need to organize your space and organize your time, making sure you keep track of all your appointments and commitments. You can also work in an organized way so you are more efficient and get more things done in a shorter period of time. Being organized can reduce stress and anxiety, making you feel more in control of your day to day activities.

Part 1

Organizing your Space

1. Organize your bedroom. To keep your space organized, start by focusing on your bedroom. Go through each item in your bedroom and determine if you can get rid of any items you no longer use or need. Reduce clutter in your bedroom and clean it out so you feel more organized and keep only items you use in your bedroom.

- For example, you may have a bookshelf in your bedroom that is stuffed full of books. Go through your books and put ones you no longer read or need in a box. Try to get rid of any books you honestly do not think you will read again. You can then donate the books in the box to charity so they are out of your room.

2. Keep your home office and your desk organized. If you have a home office or a desk, tackle this area and keep it organized. Go through all papers and bills on your desk. Put these items in folders or in a filing cabinet. Get rid of any papers you do not need to keep as hard copies. Put office supplies in drawers or cabinets. Place pens and pencils in a pen holder.

- You should also position items that you use often closer to your workspace so they are within reach. For example, if you often use a stapler in your office, keep it in the top drawer of your desk so it's within reach and you know where it is at all times.

- Organize electrical cords in your office by using zip ties to keep cords wrapped. This will prevent them from getting tangled and messy.

3. Organize your kitchen. Your kitchen will likely be one of the most used areas in your home. Keep it organized by going through each item and donating any items you no longer use or are broken, such as broken kitchen tools or old utensils. Clear out these items and then assess the items you are keeping.

- Place items together in drawers or cupboards, such as all coffee mugs together or all utensils together. Keep your kitchen counters free of items when possible and only leave out items you use often, such as a large cutting board or a kettle.

- Some items need layout or ordering rather than just grouping. Frequently used unique items, like spices, should be kept handy and accessible, such as on a spice rack on the counter.

- Perishable items, like food, should be consumed on a first-in, first-out basis. Load stacks of perishable items, such as canned food, starting with the oldest first in a cupboard or a pantry.

4. Keep your closet organized. Another spot that tends to get messy is your closet, especially if you have a lot of clothing. Organize your closet by going through your clothing and getting rid of any items you no longer wear. Often, if you haven't worn the item in one year, you can get rid of it. Group items of clothing together, such as all jeans on one shelf or all jackets hung in the same spot in your closet.

- Rotate items that are within reach in your closet so you wear different items and get the most out of each item.

- Keep all shoes together, preferably on a shoe rack or in labeled bins. This way you can view each pair and know exactly what you have in your closet.

5. Clean your space regularly. To maintain your organization, do regular cleanings of your bedroom, your home office, your desk, your kitchen, and your closet. Designate one day a week as cleaning day and do a good clean of these spots. This will ensure you reduce any clutter that accumulates in each area of your home. It will also make it easier for you to maintain the system you have in place in each area to keep them organized.

- You can also clean each space periodically throughout the week to maintain them. Do a light dusting of your home once a day. Throw out any papers or bills you don't need right away, rather than let them clutter up your space.

Part 2

Organizing your Time

1. Put important dates in a calendar. Get a calendar and hang it in a spot where you can look at it everyday, such as in your kitchen, by your bed, or in your home office. You can also put a calendar

on your computer desktop or use the Calendar App on your iPhone. Put all important dates in the calendar, such as due dates, appointments, and meetings. Keep it updated regularly to help you organize your time.

- Make it habit to check the calendar daily, such as first thing in the morning or before you go to bed at night.

- Color code items in your calendar by priority. For example, you may highlight important dates in red and less important dates in yellow.

- If you are using a Calendar App on your phone, you can set reminders days or a few hours in advance so you don't forget an important date. You can also use other organizing Apps on your phone like 24me, Quip, and Wanderlust.

2. Use a day planner. A day planner is another great way to keep your time organized. It will break down the week by day, allowing you to put in appointments or meeting down for each day. It is especially useful if you have a lot of commitments throughout the day. Write down all of your commitments by hour in the day planner. Check the planner at the start of your day so you know what you have scheduled and can stay organized.

- For example, you may write down a meeting in the morning, a phone call with a client in the afternoon, and a deadline in the evening.

3. Keep a to-do list. To stay organized, make a to-do list. You may have one list for short term things you have to do and one list for long term things you have to do. Write the to-do list on a whiteboard and keep it somewhere you can see it, such as in your kitchen or your bedroom. Cross out items as you complete them so you feel productive and motivated to tackle more items on the list.

- If you'd prefer to keep the to-do list on your computer, make a spreadsheet and use it as a to-do list. Keep the spreadsheet on your desktop so you can look at it and cross off items as you complete them.

- For example, you may have a list of short term to-do items like complete assignment for tomorrow, clean room, and order supplies for the week. You can then keep a list of long term to-do items like apply for college in one month, learn Arabic, and plan a trip.

4. Reward yourself for staying organized. To help motivate you to stay organized, use a rewards system. You may treat yourself to a baked good or lunch at your favorite restaurant when you check an item off your to-do list. Or you may give yourself a five minute break and go for a walk if you complete the items in your calendar or day planner early.

- You can also reward yourself with fun activities or relaxing activities, such as playing your favorite video game or watching your favorite show. Only give yourself these rewards when you have completed the necessary tasks for the day.

Part 3

Working in an Organized Way

1. Make a daily schedule. To stay organized while you work, create a daily schedule of tasks. List each task by importance and check them off as you complete them. Put the most important tasks first, followed by the least important. Doing this can help you feel organized on a daily basis, whether you are at work or at school.

- For example, you may list tasks like completing an assignment or preparing lunch for your children first. Then, you may schedule in time to read emails or catch up on the news, followed by other tasks in the afternoon and evening.

2. Schedule breaks throughout your work day. Though it is important that you get all of the necessary tasks done, you should also set aside time for short breaks. You may schedule in five minute breaks after every few tasks so you can stretch your legs, go for a short walk, or do a few light exercises. You may also use the breaks to get coffee or a snack.

- Having breaks will ensure you do not get too worn out or overworked, especially if you have a lot of tasks to complete for the day. If you are really busy, try to schedule at least one break in the day so you are not working too many hours straight.

3. Multitask. Another way you can work in a more organized way is to multitask, where you switch between several tasks at once. Multitasking can allow you to get multiple things done within a short period of time. It can also help you be more organized, as you will feel less overwhelmed or stressed about the things you need to get done if you complete them all at once.

- For example, you may put the kettle on for your tea and fold towels, send emails, and load the washing machine while the water boils. Or you may set a download on your computer at work and do paperwork or other tasks in the office while you wait for the download to finish.

- Just keep in mind that some studies have shown that multitasking may diminish one's ability to focus on one thing at a time.

4. Delegate tasks to others, when needed. If you have a lot to get done, try to delegate tasks to others when you can. You may delegate tasks to workers in your office or to other family members in your home. Delegating tasks can make your day run more efficiently and allow you to stay organized.

- For example, you may delegate chores in your home to your children or your family members so you are not the only one cleaning and maintaining the house. Or you may delegate tasks to coworkers who have free time or an hour to spare so you can ensure all your tasks get done for the day.

How to be Organised and Smart

Have you ever wanted to be like those honor students that have these really organized areas and backpacks? This might just be the guide you need to be more organized.

Steps

1. Keep a planner: This can be your school planner of one from any local store. I recommend colour-coding your planner. For example, with a red pen you can mark all your test dates. With pencil you can write your homework down. This really helps when you are taking a quick look at your planner. Carry it around with you where ever you go,so you can write any event down. This can help you not forget any homework.

2. Keep sticky notes. You can use these in your textbooks and on your planner to remember anything. Again I recommend using sticky notes with different colours. It can help.

3. Have a role-model which is smart and productive. This can help you stay motivated.

4. Go to the library and take out book you are interested in.Reading can help in many ways.

5. Follow a study and homework routine. That way, you could catch up on your missed out lessons daily, read in advance for the next lecture and finish your homework right away.

How to be a very Organized Person

If you will re-evaluate on how organized you actually are, will you give yourself a 5 out of 5 or a 1 out of 5? Either way, if you want to at least push yourself into being more organized, here are a few ways to help.

Steps

1. Make a To-Do list every day! Make it full of *everything* you need to do. Exclude the typical things like "wake up" or "brush your teeth" because it is already a routine for you, unless it isn't.

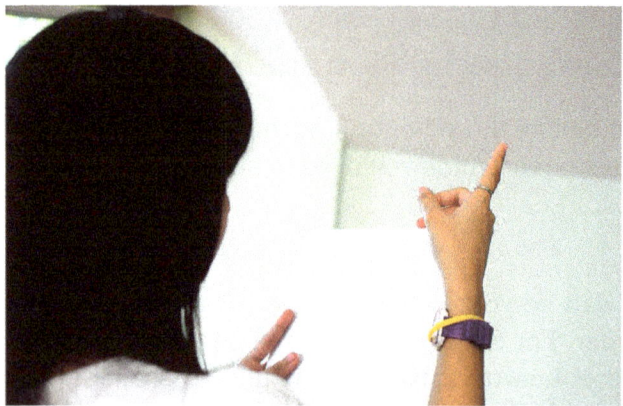

2. Follow that To-Do list. Complete *everything* on it. If you decide not to do it, then cross it out and put it on the list for tomorrow.

3. Take everything out of your room and clean it. When you put everything back in, make sure to put it in the right place so it is organized. However, you must maintain a clean and orderly room because you can't have an organized life if your room isn't.

4. Remember to put everything back where it goes whenever you take it out so you know where everything is. If you can't remember where to place things often, try to label that area so that it will remind you until you know where to place everything like the back of your hand.

5. Carry an agenda book or notebook with you at all times. If you think of something important, you can write it down. Things such as homework, chores and your other schedules are the best things to write down.

6. Keep everything up and never give up. It will not be easy, but with patience, you will surely be able to be organized. Good luck!

How to be Organized at Work

We all know being organized at work is important, but it's an ongoing struggle for many people. Believe it or not, staying organized is not as daunting as it may seem. A few quick fixes and some ongoing solutions make it easier than you might have ever thought.

Method 1

Managing your Space and Time

1. Monitor your activities. Spend a couple days keeping a journal or log of your daily activities. This will help you see exactly what you do that you might not even realize, and it will provide an initial glimpse into organizational and productivity gaps. This exercise should also be done with your big-picture goals in mind. Through the activity log, you can see what activities might be time-wasters and which activities might actually further your goals.

2. Determine your productivity times. Some of us are morning people, and some of us cringe at the idea of mornings. You might already have a sense of what times of day you're most productive. Whether you prefer evenings, mornings, lunchtime, or right before or after workday rush hours, take advantage of those times to maximize your productivity.

3. Prioritize your tasks. We all know that some tasks are more important than others, but we don't always prioritize them accordingly. So develop a ranking system by flagging or starring important tasks, for example, and be honest and flexible. Use reminders, either through a digital calendar or through sticky notes on your computer or desk. Devote more of your time and energy to top-priority items on your list. Examples include time-sensitive tasks such as things due by end of business or tomorrow. You might also prioritize responding to clients, bosses, or anyone else who pays the bills. And if you're not sure about the sensitivity or importance of a task, it's always good to ask.

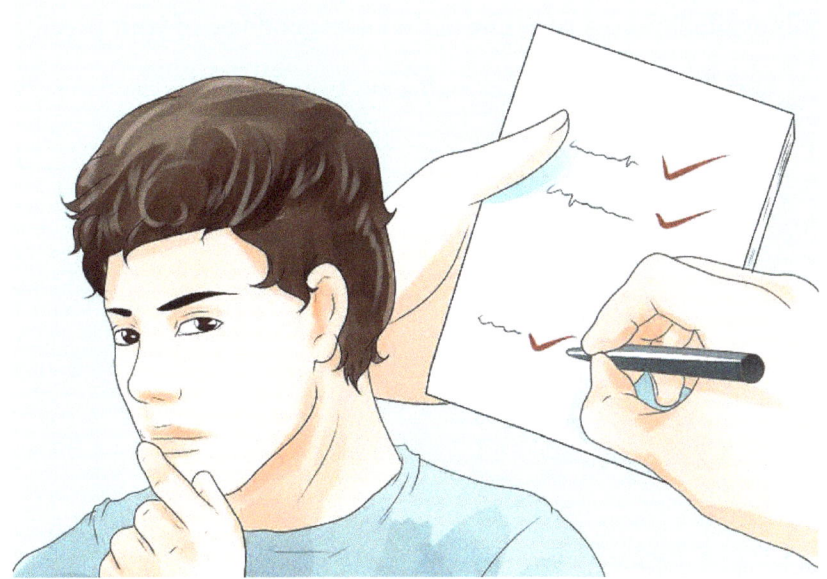

4. Knock out quick tasks right away. Not all tasks need to be prioritized and scheduled for a future completion time. Some tasks take nearly as much time to plan for or schedule as they take to accomplish. If that's the case and you can bang out those tasks right away, by all means do it! Handling quick tasks immediately also helps prevent procrastination.

5. Manage clutter and work materials. Our desks easily go from cluttered to tornado sites, obviously hampering organization. Some people even operate on a clean-desk-only policy. While that's not absolutely necessary, take steps to clear your workspace.

- Declutter. Toss your junk in the garbage and file your needed materials systematically. Clear clutter whenever possible: during lulls in the workday, breaks, or in between tasks.

- Clean up after yourself immediately. That way it's on the top of your mind. Plus, you avoid the inevitable agitation of having current clutter become part of your future clutter.

- Keep necessary supplies handy. Not everything around you is clutter, of course. Having needed tools available saves you time and makes good use of your precious space.

6. Schedule activities and appointments. Some people schedule only meetings, but not activities on their to-do list. Scheduling the most important tasks as well as appointments can be helpful. You might also "batch" your days by having meetings only on Tuesdays and Thursdays, for example. Keep some holes in your schedule as well for creative time to yourself or to accommodate the unexpected.

- Use an organizer and calendar. These can be pen-and-paper organizers, or they could be software-based calendars and personal assistant apps, such as iCalendar or Google Now.

- Categorize your activities. Categorizing or color-coding activities can give you a quick visual reminder of what's important where. For example, categories might include correspondence, projects, events, meetings, brainstorms, and even breaks or exercise and gym time.

- Streamline your technology. Online organizers and email platforms such as Outlook, for example, can combine your to-do lists, calendars, and addresses. This not only boosts your efficiency but helps streamline your thinking.

- Delegate wherever possible. In the madness of the workday, it's easy to forget that you don't have to do everything yourself. Delegate to an assistant or, if you're particularly swamped, ask a colleague to do you a solid and help you with a particular task. You can always repay them later when things slow down.

Method 2

Tackling email Systematically

1. Check email at scheduled times. Not all of us have to be glued to our inbox, as many messages aren't actually as time sensitive as we may think. If you work in a job that doesn't require immediate email follow-up, check your email at scheduled times only about three to four times per day.

2. File emails. Use filing folders and flags to your advantage instead of letting messages pile up in your inbox. Folders and subfolders in Outlook, for example, or Gmail's labels and multiple inboxes

can be an asset. If you're a journalist, for example, your folders might be called Current Stories, Future Stories, Old Stories, Interviews & Sources, and Pitches & Ideas.

- Delete and archive. Archive important, old correspondence, and delete the rest. In the example above, "Old Stories" is the journalist's archive folder. Once you start deleting old emails, you'll be surprised at how many emails are more worthy of the trashcan than the filing cabinet. Some people also swear by "inbox zero," which means having zero unread emails (or zero emails in your inbox, period). In addition to using folders and labels, you can achieve inbox zero by using your archive feature, deleting old emails during downtime, and using email decluttering apps.

3. Employ other forms of communication when more efficient. Sometimes a quick phone call can do the work of 10 back-and-forth emails. If so, make the call! If you know an email exchange merits a discussion or will involve considerable back-and-forth, sometimes it's better to have a phone call. You will often get more detail over the phone, while you and the other party to the discussion avoid drafting lengthy, time-consuming emails. You might even email a colleague and say, "I have a lot of questions for you on this. Maybe a call would be easier. Can I ring you in 5?"

4. Limit interruptions. While strategic breaks are helpful, interruptions during your work times are not. Interruptions can slow you down, break up your work rhythm, and make you lose your train

of thought. So, try using away messages and voicemail when you know you'll be too busy. These tools aren't just for when you're not physically in the office; they can be used when you're just too swamped. Many people also have an "open door policy," but you don't actually have to keep your door open at all times. You might even leave a friendly note on the door saying, "Conference Call in Progress" or "Occupied. Drop back later or email please."

5. Utilize the cloud. Cloud computing is worth considering because it can be cheaper, scalable, more efficient, and more easily updated. Content available in the cloud is particularly useful because you can access it across your devices: computers, tablets, smartphones, etc. Cloud storage also serves as a useful primary or secondary form of digital backup. Check with your IT manager or software provider because you might already have a certain amount of free disk space available in the cloud or available for a small annual fee.

6. Use bookmarks online. The major browsers all have bookmarking capabilities where you can save and organize your favorite or most frequently visited web addresses for quick and easy access. Take advantage of them so you don't forget important sites to check for news or industry updates.

Method 3

Using Time to your Advantage

1. Avoid multitasking. All the experts seem to agree on this one. While it may sound speedy or look cool on TV, multitasking is not efficient and can actually hurt your organizational effectiveness. Instead, devote your full attention to one task at a time, handle it, and move on to the next item on your list.

2. Create a schedule or timetable for yourself. Thankfully, most jobs don't require scheduling everything in your day down to the minute. However, keeping a basic schedule of the highlights and most important tasks and events of your day can help keep you on task.

  • Set time limits for certain activities. Some tasks do not require set time limits, but others should have time parameters to boost your productivity. Think of tasks throughout your day that tend to take more time than necessary, and give them time limits in the future.

- Budget extra time for other activities. Some tasks, as you've learned from experience, wind up usually taking more time than expected, but that's not necessarily a bad thing. For these types of activities, and for particularly important events and meetings, for example, budget extra time before and after.

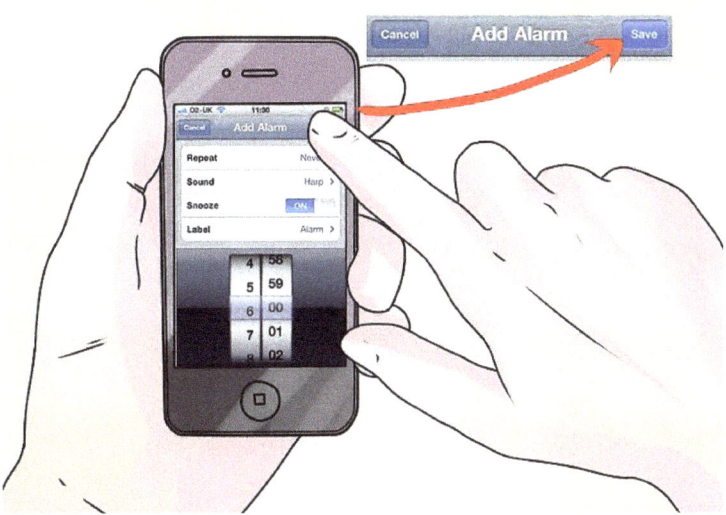

3. Use a timer app, stopwatch, or alarm clock. These can be effective tools when used sparingly. Some people like to set their alarms 10, 15, or 30 minutes ahead of time to give them advance warning or buffer time before an activity. You can also set reminder alerts.

4. Avoid postponing activities. Ask yourself if postponing is absolutely necessary or if this urge is just an example of procrastination. If you sense the latter, don't postpone—power through! However, in cases when postponing all or part of an activity is unavoidable, be sure to make note of where you left off, and reschedule with concrete plans. Alternatively, you might come up with a contingency plan. For example, if you have to cancel an in-person meeting, perhaps you can hold a conference call or web conference instead.

Method 4

Staying Healthy Physically and Mentally

1. Take breaks. Mental downtime is important to our productivity and healthy for the mind. We get so caught up in our work sometimes that we don't stop to take much-needed breaks. Taking breaks gives us needed rest that improves our productivity, but it also gives us the opportunity to take a step back and ask whether or not what we've been doing is the most efficient use of our time.

2. Sleep Better. Without proper sleep, you might feel groggy, tired, or lethargic the next day, which can harm your schedule and efficiency at work. Aim for seven to eight hours of uninterrupted sleep per night.

3. Don't compare yourself to co-workers. Most of our coworkers' jobs are different from our own, and everyone has different methods of organization that work for them. A method that makes sense and is efficient to a colleague might not be the best method for you and vice versa.

4. Accept that organization is an ongoing process. Don't expect to be perfect. Organization is ongoing and requires ongoing attention. You won't be optimally organized every day, but a little organization goes a long way to boosting your efficiency.

How to Conserve your Time

Do you have trouble conserving your energy or time? Do you feel you have no motivation to complete any tasks when you get home from work or school? Then spend some time reading this article for a few helpful tips.

Steps

1. Stretch and plan out your day. This way, you don't have to stop in the middle of the day, and contemplate what you need to fix.

2. Complete the least favorite or most difficult task on the list first. That way, you will end up being more motivated for whatever more the day might bring.

3. Maintain a clear thought pattern. Make sure you are still positive and think about how close you are to finishing your tasks and how good it feels.

4. During short walking periods, observe every object around you and imagine every detail. It helps you to remember how things should and could be.

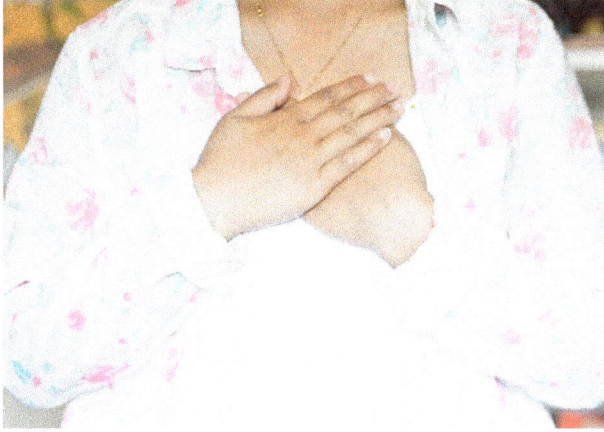

5. During times when stressed, simply stop everything and breath. No one works good when they are in distress or the bad type of pressure. Don't think irrationally and be blinded by your anger. No work is good without your heart in it.

6. Focus on every breath.

7 Focus on nothing but the present.

8. Keep yourself busy, no matter what.

9. Have a goal/reward to look forward to throughout the day.

How to Organize your Time Wisely

We've all heard the complaints that there just aren't enough hours in the day to accomplish everything that needs to get done. A few basic organizational and time management skills can help you maximize the time you do have. Learn how to organize your time wisely to get more done in the time you have.

Method 1

Identifying How You Spend Your Time

1. Keep track of daily activities. Monitor what you do on a daily basis and make a note of how much time you spend doing it. You might be surprised by how much time you actually waste throughout the day when compared to the actual amount of work you get done.

   • Remember to also keep track of mundane tasks, like making breakfast, cleaning the house, showering, etc.

2. Log all of your activities in a notebook. Once you have figured out what you do each day and how much time you spend doing it, write it into a notebook. Putting all of this information into one place and seeing it on one page will allow you to identify patterns and, potentially, areas where you may be wasting your time.

- Be comprehensive and clear when making entries into this notebook. Don't conflate separate events into one entry, don't overlook minor tasks, and be sure to write out exact times when assessing how your day breaks down.

- It can be helpful to categorize certain types of activities. For example, write household chores in blue, work activities in red and leisure activities in black. This will help you visualize how your time is being spent.

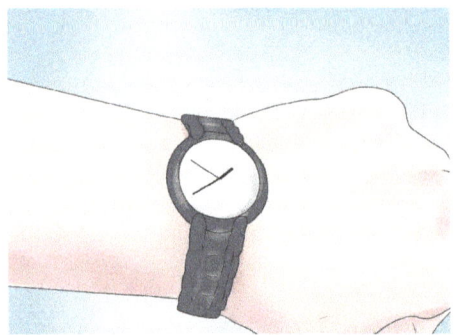

3. Assess how your time is spent. An hour a day spent zoning out? 2 hours to decide where to eat? 8 hours surfing the internet? Look for patterns in how you spend your time and determine what is necessary and what it is not.

- Do you waste time because you lack self-control? Do you procrastinate too often? Do you take on too much responsibility? These are all questions you need to ask yourself while assessing how you spend your time.

- You may find that you break up activities throughout your day in ways that don't make sense. For example, it is probably not wise to work for a half hour, then spend 10 minutes dealing with trivial matters, just to come back to work for another half hour. You will be more focused and productive if you just work for an hour and deal with trivial matters at a later time.

- It is best to attack your tasks by "chunking". Chunking is a method in which you dedicate a predetermined amount of time to a single task without distractions.

4. Consider adjustments. Now that you know exactly where and to what your time goes, start making active adjustments to your schedule. Make sure you identify areas that can't or shouldn't

be reduced simply for time concerns. Just because something takes a long time doesn't mean it is time wasted.

5. If you spend 3 hours a day sending work-related emails, it is unlikely you will be able to reduce the amount of time spent on this activity. However, if you are sending four or five personal emails between the work emails, you can definitely reduce the amount of time you dedicate to emails.

6. Change your habits and norms. Whatever your time management problem may be, there is a solution. Once you have decided where you waste time or how you should be spending your time, you will need to make a concerted effort to change your time management habits.

- If you are spending too much time cleaning your house or cooking your meals, considering hiring domestic help like a maid or a cook. For some people, their time is more valuable than their money.

- Maybe you spend a good chunk of your day surfing the internet aimlessly. You can restrict your access to the certain internet sites or social networking accounts when you are supposed to be working on something else.

Method 2

Avoiding Distractions

1. Identify distractions in your life. The biggest threats to spending your time wisely are consistent distractions. You will want to figure out what types activities or which individuals tend to end up wasting your time. Whether it is a friend who just doesn't stop talking or a guilty pleasure that draws you away from work, you can find ways to avoid these time wasters.

- If you spend a large chunk of your time on something that produces no desirable outcomes for you, it is likely just a distraction in your life that should be avoided.

- Working in an office setting, you are likely to see many of your co-workers as distractions. Be sure to avoid small talk or worthless chit chat when you are on the clock. However, keep in mind that your attitude in the office is as important to your career advancement as time management skills, so don't be rude.

2. Avoid long phone conversations. If you find you are spending a good amount of your time locked into long phone conversations, then you need to adjust your phone habits. Often times, you can achieve more in face to face meetings than you can on the phone- so cut out the long phone conversations.

- Many phone discussions, especially at the beginning or the end of the conversation, include superfluous and unnecessary conversations. People tend to lose focus and wander while on the phone, so be cognizant of that. Holding meetings in person provides more of an imperative to deal exclusively with work-related issues. This is because neither party is surrounded by distractions when a face-to-face meeting takes place.

3. Don't surf the web excessively. Many people use the internet as critical tool to accomplish the tasks they need to get done. However, just as many people are guilty of drifting over to useless news articles, sports highlights, and pictures of celebrities, kittens or puppies. Stay focused when you are on the internet. There are programs available that will block certain applications, websites and domains that can help reduce internet-related distractions.

- Avoid Facebook, Twitter, and other social networking sites when you are supposed to be focused on something else.

- Googling various topics is also a dangerous time-waster. You may think you are just going to look up one quick thing and before you know it, you have been searching the vast depths of the internet for over 3 hours.

4. Employ a "Do Not Disturb" sign. You are probably familiar with the sign you hang on your hotel room door. This sign can be equally effective in an office or workplace as well. You can get a sign like this by taking it from the next hotel you stay at, or you can print your own and attach it to the door of your work space when needed. This will eliminate the small talk that distracts you from your work.

- If you work from home, it is critical to have a dedicated work space of your own. Don't work in the common areas of your house, as the T.V., phone, or video game machine can easily distract you away from your work.

5. Make time for unavoidable distractions. There are some distractions some people just can't avoid. Sometimes it is your boss who wants to take time out of your day for a social chat or maybe an elderly family member that consistently needs help with simple tasks. Whatever these unavoidable distractions may be, if you plan for them in advance, they will not take critical time away from other projects and activities that need to get done.

Method 3

Using your Time Efficiently

1. Write everything down. Don't rely on your memory to get you through the tasks you need to get done. Write everything you need to do down in one spot and be prepared to reference this list often in order to achieve all of your goals.

- Even if a task seems minor or mundane, write it down. Your daily planner should be filled with small comments like "Call Steve," "Look up profit margins" or "Email boss."

- Make sure you carry a notepad with you at all times and write down tasks as they come up. You think you will remember to write them down later, but you may not.

2. Utilize a calendar. The simple addition of a daily calendar or planner to your set of organizational tools will help you organize time efficiently. Write down every new deadline, assignment or meeting that gets added to your schedule. Take time each morning to review your calendar for the day so you know what's ahead of you.

3. Avoid double-committing. Organize your schedule by avoiding overbooking yourself or committing yourself to too many projects or events at once. Check your calendar before agreeing to anything to verify that the time needed is free. This will keep your time organized and keep you in touch with your regular schedule.

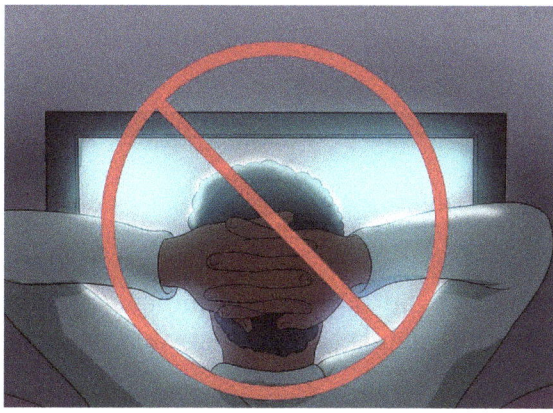

4. Omit distractions. Organize your time productively by removing elements that could be distractions or cause you to get off track and behind schedule. Keep the television and video game system

out of the area where you study or do the bills so you will focus on the tasks that need to be done first and save the fun stuff for later.

5. Prioritize your tasks. Manage your time wisely by planning to accomplish the most important or time-sensitive tasks first. Note these in your schedule with a special color highlighter or a small sticker. Schedule these top-priority tasks first to give yourself enough time to complete them, then work on less time-sensitive things around the prioritized ones.

- Be ready to change your priorities from time to time. Things do come up last minute and will require your immediate attention. You will have to stop what you are doing and refocus your energy and time on this last minute objective from time to time. Just be sure it does not occur too often.

- If you find yourself consistently rearranging your priorities throughout the day, something is wrong. While minor adjustments to one's schedule can be expected, having to make consistent adjustments probably means you are not prioritizing properly in the first place.

6. Be realistic. Allow yourself a realistic amount of time to complete each task. If you think something will take between a half hour and an hour to complete, give yourself the full hour. Being realistic about how long something will take will prevent you from getting overwhelmed or behind schedule.

- It is always safer to err on the side of caution and give yourself more time than you will need. If you finish your task early, you will be free to move on to the next task- which ultimately should not impact your productivity.

7. Schedule the basics. Remember to include times for the everyday basics, like eating and showering, in your schedule. These might seem like second nature, but it's important to allow time for them among your other scheduled tasks to ensure that you don't skip them and that they don't put you behind schedule.

8. Use a reminder system. Use simple reminders in addition to your daily planner to help remember important tasks or deadlines. Use sticky notes or voice or text alerts on your cell phone at certain times to remind yourself to do something or that you have something scheduled. This backup system will help keep you from forgetting things.

- Avoid relying on other people to remind you about something. They are just as likely to forget it as you are.

- If something is extremely important, arrange multiple reminders for yourself. You can overlook a single sticky note or phone alert.

9. Ask for help. Ask someone else for help and delegate smaller tasks if needed. It will benefit your schedule overall if you swallow your pride and ask someone to pitch in with a few small chores around the house or with taking care of dinner on a busy weeknight.

- Make sure you delegate responsibilities to qualified people. Someone getting the work done is not enough. You want them to get the work done well.

- Don't make a habit of pawning off your work others. It does not reflect good time management skills. It just makes you look lazy and unmotivated.

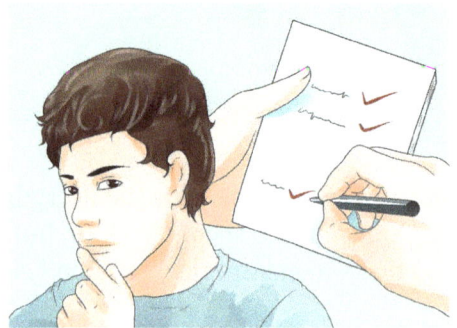

10. Gauge your productivity. From time to time, it is necessary to take a step back and analyze what you accomplished, how well you performed, and how much time it took. Taking stock of these aspects of your work and life can help you make changes to your schedule and daily pattern of operation, producing surprisingly effective results.

11. Reward yourself. Working too hard or too often can lead to a burnout, making it difficult to focus on even the simplest tasks. So, take some time to celebrate what you have accomplished from time to time and reward yourself with something you truly enjoy.

- Make sure your down time is dedicated to enjoying yourself. Turn off your work phone and avoid answering emails. If you are mixing work with your leisure time, you really aren't rewarding yourself or avoiding burn out.

- If you work Monday to Friday, take the weekend off. If you have been working for three months straight on one project, take a brief vacation when you are finished with it.

How to be Punctual

Showing up late to every meeting and event can stress you out and leave others questioning how reliable you are. You'd probably love to be on time whenever and wherever you go, but punctuality doesn't come naturally to everyone. The good news is you can train yourself to be on time, every time, by changing your habits and your views about punctuality. See Step 1 and beyond to learn quick tricks and long-term strategies for being more punctual.

Method 1

Using Tricks to Get Out the Door Quickly

1. Have everything ready the night before. If you're not sure why you seem to chronically late, take a look at what happens before you leave the house. You probably set aside a certain amount of time to get ready to go, and end up scrambling to get through a checklist of tasks before you can leave. If you have everything ready to go well in advance, though, you won't have a bunch of hurdles standing between you and getting where you need to go. Every single night, go through the following routine so that you'll have a lot less to do in the morning:

- Lay out the clothes you're going to wear.

- Complete any tasks you might normally leave for the morning, like writing emails or printing out documents.

- Pack up your bag or briefcase with everything you'll need the next day.

- Have everything ready so you can make a quick breakfast, or eliminate the need for morning cooking altogether by making some overnight oats.

2. Keep your essentials near the door. Many people who are often late spend too much time searching around for their keys, cell phone, charger or wallet. If you keep all of your essential items in the same drawer or tray near the door, they'll be waiting there for you when it's time to leave.

- If you tend to walk in the door and leave your keys on the counter, your wallet in the bedroom, and your phone on the kitchen table, you'll spend too much extra time looking for everything when you could be on your way. Every once in a while, you'll probably forget an important item and have to go back to retrieve it, making you even later.

- Instead, the moment you walk in the door, empty your pockets of all your essential items and put them in the same place every time. If you keep everything in your purse, put that in the same spot in your house every time, too.

3. Create a staging area near the door. As you go about your daily routine around the house and think of items that you will need for your next trip, take the time to set them in the staging area. If you get in the habit of doing this, everything will be ready to go and you will not have to do the mental inventory countdown each time you are ready to go.

- You can go even further and put the items in your car as you think of them.

4. Anticipate delays before they happen. Are you full of excuses that seem legitimate? *Traffic was bad.* Or, *The train got delayed.* Worse, *I had to stop and get gas.* If you thought ahead and anticipated these everyday delays, they wouldn't be making you late all the time.

- Anticipate that these things are going to happen fairly often. Being on a stalled subway car is not a once-in-a-lifetime experience. Leave early enough to overcome unanticipated delays and still get there on time.

- Avoid completely unnecessary delays like stopping for gas. Fill your car the night before. Make sure your subway pass is loaded with plenty of fare, and eat at home, instead of stopping at the fast food drive-through for breakfast and waiting in line.

- Check traffic and the weather to see if anything might hold you up, and leave early enough to make up for any anticipated extra travel time. Remember, too, that the possibility of delays in bad weather is high. Leave a sufficient time buffer to absorb the worst typical delay.

- In cold weather allow an extra five or ten minutes to clear frost, snow, and ice from your vehicle.

- If you ride a bus, know the route, have your fare, and keep cab money on hand in case of emergency.

- If you are depending on another person for a ride—have a plan B!

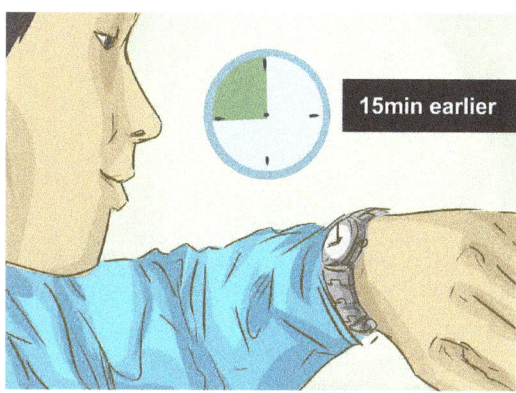

5. Commit yourself to being 15 minutes early for everything. If you have to be to work at 8:00, don't even tell yourself you can walk in the door right on the dot. Instead, say to yourself, "I have to be at work at 7:45." If you do this, you will be on time even with little unforeseen interruptions. You will be on time even if you encounter a traffic jam. And on those rare times that you actually show up 15 minutes early; you will get kudos for being an enthusiastic employee.

- If you can't stand waiting, have something you can read in short segments almost everywhere you go. This makes it easy to be early, since in the 10-15 minutes you have before an appointment/event, you can get a few pages of reading done. It'll feel like you're getting something done (and you are) while you are waiting.

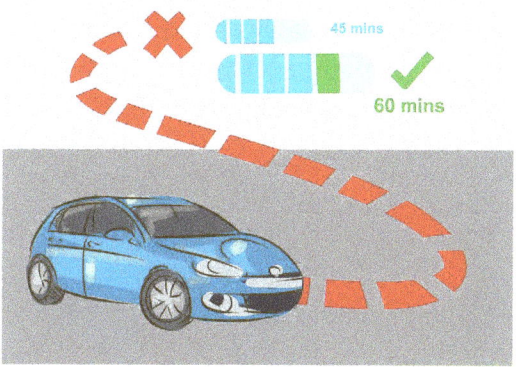

6. Overestimate the time it'll take to get there. If you tend to have everything ready to go in the morning, and you show up late even when you don't experience delays, you might be underestimating the amount of time it takes to get where you're going. Optimistic thinkers tend to shave off a few minutes, hoping they'll be able to get places faster. Unfortunately, all it does is make them late! Be realistic when you're planning your commutes, and punctuality will follow.

- Sometimes, it's hard to know exactly how long it will take to get somewhere. If you're preparing for an important meeting, like an interview, you might want to drive the route or do the train commute in advance of the meeting day. Time your trip so you'll know what time you need to leave the house.

- Don't forget to add 15 minutes to the overall trip time to account for delays. If you figure it'll take 40 minutes to get to your meeting site, leave 55 minutes early just in case something trips you up.

Method 2

Forming Better Habits

1. Get up the second your alarm goes off. Don't hit the snooze button, linger in bed, and watch TV at the very start of your day. You probably didn't factor in an extra 10 or 15 minutes in bed when you planned out what time you'd need to wake up in the morning in order to get to your scheduled events on time. By getting up late you are setting a pattern of lateness for the rest of the day. Those extra minutes in bed will add up and push everything else back, so get up as quickly as you can.

- Try stretching, splashing your face with water, and brushing your teeth right away to wake your body up more quickly.

- If you can't get out of bed on time, you may be going to bed too late. Go to sleep earlier to see if that helps. This makes it a lot easier to get up on time and helps you stay on task during the day. Unless you know otherwise, assume you need eight hours of sleep every night.

2. Re-examine how long your daily tasks really take. For example, you might be under the impression that you take a 15 minute shower, assuming that starting at 6:30 you can leave at 6:45. But, what about the time you spend before and after the actual shower? It's quite possible you really spend 20 or even 30 minutes in the bathroom, and that's why you can never leave by 6:45. So, think about the things you do every day, and try to keep an estimate of how long it takes you.

- Time yourself a few days in a row to see how long it actual takes you to perform certain tasks. Use a stopwatch and record the times over the course of a week, then average the times so you'll have an accurate indication of how much time to plan for each activity.

3. See where you often waste the most time. What do you get caught up doing that prevents you from getting out the door? "Time sinkholes," like getting distracted while checking emails, spending too long curling your hair, or stopping at a coffee shop on the way to work are often unnoticed by us, and can throw off daily planning.

- When you discover a sinkhole, try to change your habits around the activity to make it faster. For example, standing up while quickly checking your emails makes it hard to lose an hour randomly surfing the web.

4. Change the time on your watch. Set the time 5 minutes earlier than the actual time. This means you should always be at least 5 minutes early for an event or meeting.

5. Make a note of where you should be in regards to time. For instance, if you have to leave your house at 8 for work, tell yourself, "It's 7:20, I should be getting in the shower." "It's 7:35, I should

be brushing my teeth." This will help keep you on track. It is useful to think up a morning schedule to get used to this habit.

- Consider printing out a schedule you can reference throughout the morning. Post it up in your bedroom, office, kitchen, and other places where you'll be sure to see it.

6. Don't overbook yourself. Maybe you're often late because you schedule back-to-back appointments without leaving enough time in between to move from place to place. Examine your schedule and make sure each activity is buffered by several minutes before and after so you can spend that time traveling, resting, eating, and doing other things you need to do between appointments.

7. Surround yourself with timepieces. If you tend to space out and forget what time it is, you probably need more clocks in your life. If you don't like wearing a watch, have your cellphone on hand at all times. Wall clocks are attention-grabbers that help people stay on task, too. Make sure all your clocks are set to the same time, so you don't get confused.

- Utilize timers, alarms and reminders throughout the day as well. For example, you might want to set your phone to vibrate or ring when you have 10 minutes to go before your next class or meeting.

- Some people intentionally set their clocks several minutes fast in order to trick themselves into getting to places early. You could try this to see if it works for you, but many people find that they just mentally adjust their concept of what time it is to account for the extra minutes, and they end up late anyway. Knowing what time it really is will help you stay grounded and punctual.

Method 3

Changing your Attitude about Punctuality

1. Acknowledge that you have a hard time being punctual. If you have a chronic problem with punctuality, you might be prone to making a lot of excuses. Some of them might be valid, like if you're late to a meeting because you had a flat tire, or a winter storm stalled traffic for an hour. But if it seems like you're constantly trying to explain away your tardiness, it's time to own up to your problem. As with any problem, you cannot fix it if you're in denial that it's a problem at all.

- If you're not sure whether your issue is chronic, ask your friends and family to tell you honestly whether they consider you a punctual person. If punctuality is truly an issue for you, you won't have been able to hide it from them.

- Don't be too hard on yourself if you have trouble being punctual, though. According to a study conducted in San Francisco, 20 percent of the US population has the same issue.

2. Notice how being late affects others. You probably really want to be on time, and when you're late, you feel genuinely sorry for inconveniencing others. But if you're late again and again, people will feel that your behavior is inconsiderate. Being late puts other people in the position of having to wait for you. It's seen as a statement that you value your time more than you value theirs, even if you really don't feel that way.

- Think of how *you* feel when someone else is the one who's late for a meeting. Do you appreciate having to sit alone in a restaurant while you wait for your friend to show up half an hour late?

- Eventually, being late all the time will erode people's faith in your reliability, creating a negative impression that could eventually extend to matters other than punctuality.

3. Get your adrenaline rush in other ways. Do you feel a little buzzed when you're rushing to beat the clock? It's like a game, and if you can get there before the timer runs out, you win. However, this exhilarating habit can have bad consequences when you lose your gamble with time too often. If you like the rush of adrenaline you feel when you're down to the wire, stop putting your appointments on the line and try to get it some other way, like by playing timed computer games, taking up track and field sports, or — if you *really* like the rush — parachuting from a plane.

4. Make punctuality one of your core values. It doesn't seem as meaningful as honesty or integrity, but punctuality is intimately tied to these important values. When you say you're going to be somewhere at a certain time, and you don't show up, what does that say about you? When it happens over and over, might it affect others' impression of your integrity, or cause them to think twice about what you say? Try to take punctuality as seriously as you take other values you strive to uphold. If you care more about being punctual, you'll start being more punctual.

- Examine the areas in which you're more likely to be flippant about punctuality. If there are certain people you don't bother meeting on time, or a certain class you always come to 15 minutes late, it's possible that the people and the class just aren't that important to you.

- Try to spend your time doing things you care about doing, and do them with intention. Show up on time and be all in. When you care about what you're doing, and you're living with integrity, it feels right to get there on time.

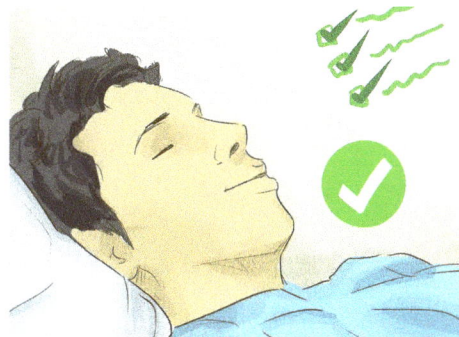

5. Enjoy the rewards of being a punctual person. After a few weeks of rearranging your habits and thought patterns so you can be more punctual, it won't feel as difficult — and you'll start reaping the rewards of being the sort of person who's never late. Here are a few examples of the benefits you'll experience:

- You'll be much less stressed out on a daily basis, and you won't have to make excuses and apologize all the time.

- You'll probably experience a professional boost, since you'll no longer be late for work.

- Your personal life will be uplifted as people begin to see you as a reliable person and trust you more.

- Being habitually punctual tends to have the effect of actually allowing you to be late from time to time, since people will start giving you the benefit of the doubt.

How to Manage Internet Time

Managing the time you spend online is vital because you want it to be time well spent. If you spend too much time online, it could affect your productivity and you might have wasted a lot of time doing nothing. How do you manage your internet time?

Steps

1. Set a time limit. This should be one that is enough to complete your task as well as spare a little time for some personal internet surfing.

2. Set your priorities. You should make sure to know which ones you'll do first. Is it your task or is it personal web browsing? Your priority number one should come first and should have more time compared to the rest.

3. Set up an alarm. Once you've decided on your time limit and you know your priorities, set up an alarm whenever you go online. As soon as the alarm goes off, logout and turn off the computer so that you won't be tempted to turn it on and spend extra hours browsing.

Overcome Procrastination

Procrastination hampers an individual's efficiency. Focusing on goals, staying motivated and avoiding distractions are effective techniques to avoid procrastination. The aspects elucidated in this chapter are of vital importance to provide a better understanding of time management.

Procrastination

Procrastination is the avoidance of doing a task that needs to be accomplished. It is the practice of doing more pleasurable things in place of less pleasurable ones, or carrying out less urgent tasks instead of more urgent ones, thus putting off impending tasks to a later time. Sometimes, procrastination takes place until the "last minute" before a deadline. Procrastination can take hold on any aspect of life—putting off cleaning the stove, repairing a leaky roof, seeing a doctor or dentist, submitting a job report or academic assignment or broaching a stressful issue with a partner. Procrastination can lead to feelings of guilt, inadequacy, depression and self-doubt.

Negative Impact

For some people, procrastination can be persistent and tremendously disruptive to everyday life. For these individuals, procrastination may be symptomatic of a psychological disorder. Procrastination has been linked to a number of negative associations, such as depression, irrational behaviour, low self-esteem, anxiety and neurological disorders such as ADHD. Others have found relationships with guilt and stress. Therefore, it is important for people whose procrastination has become chronic and is perceived to be debilitating to seek out a trained therapist or psychiatrist to see if an underlying mental health issue may be present.

Procrastination feeds powerlessness and vice versa. The behavior is paradoxical: it maximizes suffering, failures and feeds a conviction of impotence (trying incessantly, sincerely, but in vain, giving up faster and faster because of the conviction of powerlessness and the absence of immediate satisfaction). The passage to the act (and not the act itself) becomes unbearable.

With a distant deadline, procrastinators report significantly less stress and physical illness than do non-procrastinators. However, as the deadline approaches, this relationship is reversed. Procrastinators report more stress, more symptoms of physical illness, and more medical visits, to the extent that, overall, procrastinators suffer more stress and health problems.

How to Stop Procrastinating

If you're a chronic procrastinator, you know the pain and stress that comes with putting things off. Although you may have the desire to accomplish something, getting the motivation to do it is a different matter. Fortunately, overcoming your procrastination is easy to do when you put your mind to it. Side note: If you have anything due right now, and you haven't finished it, leave this article and complete that work.

Steps

1. Create a to-do list. Yes, make yourself an old fashioned to-do list with check boxes and everything. List everything, big and small, that you have to do for your entire day; break big activities into smaller bits if necessary. Then, as you work through your day, check off each of the items on your list. You will feel a growing sense of pride as you visually monitor your ever-diminishing list of projects.

- Focus your list on including the things you typically put off, not the things you are sure to do on a regular basis.

- If necessary, set time-frames for your items to be done by. For example, list "take the dog for a walk by 12:30" rather than simply "walk the dog."

- Re-evaluate your list halfway through your day to rank your items based on highest priority. Then, tackle the most important ones before looking back at the smaller things to do.

- Keep a notebook by hand before you start your workday. Write every thought down that comes up during work. Every single to do or things you want to do at that specific moment. Don't do it, put it on a list and do it later. This prevents you from getting into the "procrastination zone."

2. Finish the hard stuff. When you have a looming project that's bogging you down and making you unproductive in other areas, tackle it first. Finishing the largest item on your list of things to do will make you feel extra productive and give you the boost to do other things you've been pushing to the side.

- If your "big project" is something that can't be done in one sitting, make a list of small parts of it that you can accomplish today. Don't worry about completing the entire thing, but take steps now so that doing so in the future is a breeze.

- Make an ultimate to-do list for this single project, and have it placed somewhere you will see it on a regular basis. As you mark things off, you will be motivated to continue doing so, and seeing it on a regular basis will remind you that your project needs to be done.

3. Do two-minute tasks. Whenever you are presented with something that you don't want to do or would consider putting off, ask yourself, "will this take me less than two minutes to finish?" For many of us, this includes small chores, like taking out the trash or pulling a few weeds, but can include simple tasks in all areas of life. Anything that you want to put off but takes two minutes to do - do it. Simply force yourself to use the next 120 seconds to be productive and do the duty you normally would push off for hours or days..

4. Create a timed work frenzy. If you find yourself being pulled off into the depths of daydreams, set a period of time to do nothing but work. Take ten minutes and remove all distractions - your phone, magazines, or thoughts of your attractive love - and go into a working frenzy. Force your-self to work productively for ten minutes, and then go back to whatever it was you were doing. Chances are, you'll get into a groove and keep working at a high pace even when your frenzy time is out. Working with a timer is generally regarded by most experts as being one of the best ways to develop self-discipline and stop procrastination. The most famous method of working to strict time controls (known as time-boxing) involves creating a list of tasks. Each task is then assigned an exact amount of time to complete. If you don't finish the task in the allotted time, then you move on to the next one. Using this work arrangement, it forces you to take action, as you can't afford to waste any time. .

5. Give yourself a break. If you can't seem to focus and are working half-heartedly at your tasks, give yourself a brief break. Set a timer for ten minutes, and take a nap, read a book, or call your friend. Do whatever it is you've been daydreaming about so that the temptation is removed once you get back to work. Just be sure to follow through with your deadline rather than ignoring it when your alarm finally goes off.

6. Remove your distractions. Although it may seem like calling your mom or finishing up the next chapter in your book are things you must accomplish in the near future, they're probably just distracting you from getting your work done. Put on some noise-cancelling headphones, turn off your phone, and hide your temptations (books, your guitar, cleaning, whatever it may be).

- If you have a problem with internet surfing while you're working on your computer, try using a specialized computer app that limits your internet use. There are a range of available apps that block off certain (or all) websites for a particular amount of time that you set, and can only be voided if your computer is turned off.

- If your problem is focusing on writing a big essay or work report, try using a writing program. You can search online to find many word-processing programs that completely blocks out your screen (including the taskbar at the bottom) and plays soft instrumental music or white noise to help you concentrate. You can download the most basic version for free online.

7. Don't be a perfectionist. If you're waiting for the perfect time, the perfect supplies, or you won't stop until you've "perfected" your project, you're putting off completing your task. Avoid this "perfect" thinking by considering quantity over quality. If your project doesn't require perfection but you're still focused on it, stop and move on to your next task. When you've finished everything, you can backtrack and finish perfecting your original task.

8. Motivate yourself. Many people claim the reason they procrastinate is because they work best under pressure. So what do you do if your projects don't have any deadlines? Make your own. Set a time that you must complete your project by, and either reward yourself at the end of that time, or set up a punishment for yourself if you aren't successful in your endeavor.

- Positive reinforcement is the most effective means of motivating yourself. Give yourself a treat to look forward to as a reward for buckling down on your to-do list; go see a movie, eat a chocolate bar, go out with a friend, whatever it is that will motivate you.

- Try using negative reinforcement - taking away something bad - as a motivator. For example, promise yourself that if you finish your essay by Friday night, you won't have to run your errands, do your chores, or whatever it is that you don't want to do.

- If reinforcement isn't working for you, use punishment as a motivator. Use negative punishment - taking away something good - to try to work harder. Don't let yourself take that nap, eat your dinner, or finish your favorite book until your tasks have been done.

- For the most severe examples of procrastination, put your money on the line. Give someone you trust a certain amount of money, $50 for example, and tell them to spend it on themselves if you don't finish your project by a certain time. This way, you have to work in order to keep your hard-earned money in your own pocket.

9. Get an accomplice. If you can't seem to work on your own, find a friend or family member to help you work. You could even make a pact with a friend with the same goals to, for example, exercise

everyday, so that you feel pressured not to let them down. Have them encourage you to stay on task and help you when you need it. Telling someone about what you need to do will motivate you to finish your project, because if you don't you will have to suffer the embarrassment of admitting it to them.

- Set up a few hours of time where you go around and accomplish all your projects with a friend. This way, you will have someone with you while you work to keep you focused and on track.

- Schedule "check-ins" with your friend where they call to see where you're at. These can be deadlines for certain tasks, at which point you will either be praised or chastised by your friend based on your progress report.

10. Focus on the end goal. It's easy to see only the giant list of things to do, rather than the anxiety-free feeling of accomplishment at having finished them. As you work, focus on all the free time, relaxation, money, whatever it may be that you get when you finish. This will help you to stay on task and work towards your goal.

11. Do one task at a time. Although it seems like multitasking is doing more work in a small amount of time but multi-taskers are often inefficient and do much less work. So practice doing one thing at a time and don't overwhelm your self with tasks. Suppose we have a list of things to do. It's so much better to finish the task at hand rather than jumping to another task without completing the first one. Yes, it's true that there are many distractions which are strong enough to throw us off the track. This is because of the process called "temporal discounting" which says we are more likely to go for a reward which is more imminent than for one which is far in the future. Small rewards like TV, facebook, etc. provide us a small imminent reward.

How to Fight Procrastination

Everyone struggles with procrastination on occasion. It can be hard to begin major projects or assignments that you don't enjoy. However, there are specific techniques that you can try to fight procrastination and become more focused and productive on work, school, or home projects.

Part 1

Getting Started on your Work

1. Force yourself to begin the task. This might seem overly simplistic, but even sitting down at your desk to start a project or buying the materials needed for a home repair, for example, can help

change your mindset and fight procrastination. The old saying that getting started is half the battle is true, especially if you struggle with procrastination.

- To help yourself get started, try to make your task as enjoyable as possible. For example, if you need to sit down to file your taxes, turn on some music that you like or envision how happy you'll be once the task is complete and you don't have to worry about it anymore. (Especially if you get a refund!)

2. Eliminate your known distractions. Are you addicted to Tumblr or Pinterest? Is Netflix calling your name and taking you away from work that you need to be doing? If possible, disconnect from the internet while you work. Working with spreadsheets or other Office applications usually allows for this. If you need the internet for your project, try telling yourself that you can spend as much time watching your favorite shows as you like once the project is finished.

- If noise is a major distraction for you, then you might want to try foam earplugs or noise canceling headphones. You can find foam earplugs in any drugstore or convenience store.

3. Set concrete goals for yourself. Sometimes procrastination is the result of feeling overwhelmed with too many projects or having tasks with non-specific requirements or due dates. Self-starting can be hard. It's important to set specific, doable goals for yourself.

- For example, if you know that you have a major research paper due at the end of the semester, then it can be hard to start on it for a variety of reasons: a far away due date, no specific topic for the paper, or simply that there are more enjoyable ways to spend your time. However, if you set concrete goals like choosing a topic early on or writing a page or two a week, then the large, intimidating project that you might normally procrastinate on won't simply exist in the abstract a few months down the road. It will exist "now" and you will be less likely to procrastinate and be pulling all-nighters at the end of the semester.

4. Minimize interruptions as much as possible. When you finally do sit down to complete a task you've been procrastinating on, it can be frustrating to get interrupted repeatedly. Whether it's an inconsiderate roommate or colleague or electronic interruptions, minimizing these will help you actually be able to get to work and not procrastinate.

- Set your email client to not automatically alert you when emails arrive, and silence your phone completely. Be sure the phone is set to mute, not vibrate, as you can still hear/feel the vibrate setting and it will still distract you.

- Politely let your chatty roommate or colleague know that you are up against a deadline and have to get some work done. If you feel rude saying this, you can try softening the blow by mentioning that you can chat with then over lunch or dinner later on if they're free, but right now you have to get your work done.

5. Prioritize your work. Often, we procrastinate because we simply feel overwhelmed and don't know where to begin. To help fight procrastination, it is important to prioritize your work in order of importance and/or by deadline.

- Using a planner is helpful for this. Get one large enough to have both a weekly and monthly view so you can look ahead to future projects and visualize the deadlines for current projects.

- If you prefer, you can use the planner on your phone, tablet, or computer. If you choose to use an electronic planner, be sure to set audible alerts because these planners and calendars tend to have a smaller screen view that might not be able to show all tasks on a single screen. Play around with planner/calendar apps to find the one that works best for you and has the best interface.

6. Change your work environment. Sometimes our work environment is the reason we tend to procrastinate. If you find yourself working in the middle of a huge mess or with noisy neighbors that drive you crazy, you need to change your environment to be productive and stop procrastinating.

- Try devoting 10 minutes to do a quick "tidy" of your immediate work space. Organize papers, put away clutter, and throw out any trash. This will give you some breathing room and a small sense of accomplishment which will help you begin your work.

- If environmental factors beyond your control are the problem, then you might need to relocate your work space for the day. Good choices might be your local library or a cafe.

Part 2

Maximizing Your Productivity

1. Break tasks down into manageable sizes. Feeling overwhelmed by huge projects can cause us to simply delay starting them. Breaking down projects into smaller goals can help you stop procrastinating and get started on your work.

- For example, if you need to repaint your bedroom, all the sanding, taping, trim work, priming and painting can be very overwhelming. However, if you make a goal to sand and clean the walls one day, tape everything off and prime the walls the next day, and finally paint on the third day, your major project will become more manageable, and you'll be more likely to get started on it.

2. Try using productivity apps. There are apps and browser extensions that will block your social media or any other sites that you deem "time wasters." Check out one of these to maximize your productivity and cut down on distractions that help you procrastinate.

- Some good examples of apps and browser extensions designed to help you stay on track are StayFocusd for Google Chrome or Timeful and Pocket for Apple and Android products.

3. Take mental health breaks. Although this may seem counterproductive, breaks can help you reset and refocus. Get a snack or a cup of coffee and reflect on what you still need to do. Avoid beating yourself up for not having done more up to this point, and use your break as a refresher. Stand up, stretch, and use positive thinking to tell yourself that even though you haven't accomplished as much as you wanted up to this point, you will once you go back to work. Sometimes a short break and a personal pep talk can help you refocus and stave off procrastination.

4. Reward yourself for completing tasks. Even if your project is something you really dislike, you can help yourself get to work on it if you promise yourself something enjoyable upon its completion. You might tell yourself that you can binge watch your favorite show on Netflix or go out for a drink or some ice cream once you've completed your goal or task. Having something to look forward to can help jumpstart you and help you fight procrastination.

5. Have an accountability partner. If you have a friend or colleague who struggles with procrastination, too, then you might benefit from using each other as accountability partners. You can set up a friendly competition to see who can get further on their work, or you can simply use each other as support. Being accountable to someone will help you stop procrastinating.

- For example, if you catch your accountability partner checking Facebook during your designated work time, then you can gently remind them that they need to be working, and they can do the same for you. Be sure to be polite when you catch the other not working.

6. Set a timer to keep you on track. Try setting a timer for 10 minutes and telling yourself that for that time, you have to work as hard as you can on a project. Regardless of how large the project is, you must work on it nonstop and give it your best for 10 minutes.

- This is an effective jumpstart strategy that fights procrastination because the short time allotment is manageable and you can immediately see the results of your burst of hard work.

Part 3

Maintaining Reasonable Expectations

1. Step outside for some light exercise. It can be depressing to be indoors all day worrying about all the work you need to do. Even though it might seem counter productive, step outside and take a short 5 to 10 minute walk in the fresh air. This can help you refocus and combat procrastination. Once you come back inside, however, ensure that you go back to work.

2. Don't be hard on yourself if you procrastinate. Be kind to yourself when you're struggling with procrastination. Think about how you would treat someone else who was struggling with getting their work done. You would probably be kind and try to gently talk with them about how to go about completing their tasks. Do the same for yourself. Don't beat yourself up about procrastinating. Simply accept that you've put off your work up to this point and make a fresh start.

3. Don't drag out work till it's perfect. Our obsession with perfection can cause us to procrastinate in a roundabout way. Sometimes we'll sit down and work hard on a project only to keep revising

or fixing it until it's past its deadline. Embrace that you only need to do your best and then submit your work. Don't procrastinate submitting your work because you think it might not be perfect. It probably isn't perfect, but it can be great and ready to turn in without being perfect.

4. Be introspective. Try to identify the importance of the task at hand and determine what the consequences will be if you don't complete it. Will you receive a negative review at work for failing to complete a report or a bad grade for not writing your research paper? Objectively consider what will realistically happen if you keep procrastinating. Sometimes this bit of reflection can help you get going on a project.

• It's important to remember when doing this to be objective about the possible outcomes. If the outcome isn't especially negative, then this project or task might be one that you can delay in favor of more pressing work.

5. Consider that there might be a medical reason for your procrastination. Finally, if your procrastinating is particularly bad and accompanied by other symptoms like sadness or hyperactivity, you might benefit from talking to your doctor. ADHD, depression, and thyroid disorders are just a few of the many medical issues that can affect your ability to concentrate, focus, and be productive.

How to not Procrastinate with Homework

Do you have a problem with procrastination when doing homework? If you nodded your head, you're not alone. Most people have the same problem from time to time. Lack of motivation, failure to utilize time effectively, zero structure, the causes of procrastination are nearly endless. It's time to stop procrastinating!

Method 1

Removing Distractions and Temptations

1. Turn off social media updates. We are all plugged into the matrix today, whether it be Facebook, Twitter, Instagram, or another way to connect. Regardless of the form of social media or game, turn off updates. If you can't resist temptation, there are software tools and router settings to limit internet usage.

2. Pull in your email. Email automatically delivered to you based on receipt or software timeline is pushed, because it's sent without your interaction. When you must look or check for new email, it's called pulling email. Every email client has a setting to stop automatic email push and notification. Remove the distraction by seeing emails only when you deem necessary.

3. Shut down the TV and radio. The allure of TV and radio is stronger than homework. Hearing the opening jingle of your favorite TV show, or a great quote from an intense movie, can lead to complete distraction. It's even possible the TV and radio are subliminally distracting you.

4. Wear noise-cancelling headphones. Isolate yourself completely from sound and distraction. Noise-cancelling headphones are perfect for 100% focus on the task at hand. Choose one you believe will help you really focus.

5. Change your physical work environment. Try to make it as much like a library as possible. Bright lights will help avoid sleepiness, which can hinder motivation. Working at a desk instead of your

recliner, sofa, or bed will help you stay on task. Keep only homework related items near you. Clear off the desk or your work area so the only possible temptation is homework completion.

Method 2

Encouraging yourself to Act

1. Put pressure on yourself by making intentions public. Tell anyone who will listen you intend on finishing your homework by a specific time and ensure they hold you accountable. Assign a consequence (for you) and reward (for them) if the deadline is not met.

- Tell friends to post an embarrassing story of you online if you don't finish on time.

- Ask your mother to create a fair punishment for delaying.

- Ask your father to concoct something even more devious if you don't finish after your mother's punishment.

2. Keep track of assignments in the moment. Write down on a piece of paper (or in a planner) what homework you have or what project needs to be finished while you are still in class. When you get

home, start on it immediately! Touch the pencil to the paper or get your fingers on the home-keys. Getting started is the most difficult step.

3. Reassure yourself! The homework would not be assigned if not applicable to your class. If second-guessing or a negative thought pops into your head, it's important to focus on the positive. Imagine your future self engaging in your favorite activity, feet kicked in the air, completely relaxed because of how quickly and correctly homework was finished!

4. Reward yourself for any progress. Write a title for the report? High five yourself. Finish the first paragraph? Maybe some candy is in order. Solve a complicated math problem after several failed attempts? Pat yourself on the back and take a quick break. Positive reinforcement can be very effective if used properly.

Method 3

Creating a To-Do List

1. Plan ahead and separate your task into smaller, identifiable tasks. Lists are a great way create structure and order to goals that appear chaotic or impossible.

- Think of your list as an assembly line where each step reinforces your ability to complete the list, to focus on the importance of each task, and commit yourself to finishing the homework.

- If procrastination persists, make the tasks even smaller. Remember, every waterfall starts with a drop of water, and every marathon starts with the first step. If motivation eludes you, keep breaking things down until the first step is so simple you can't help but to succeed.

2. Do the small tasks first. Accomplishing even the most simple, mundane task is important. If you do a small task as you awaken, it's more likely to encourage further accomplishments. The same

applies to homework. Writing your name or a title, highlighting something important, creating an outline, whatever it is, doing a small portion will instill pride and lead to lead to other tasks.

3. Associate a timeline with your tasks. Without a timeline, procrastination is possible until the homework is due, or until you are forced to cram. Put the timeline requirements on your list. Integrate a calendar into your timeline and assign specific work for each day remaining before the deadline.

- A 1000-word essay due at the end of the week could be 100 words every hour if you have a lot of time, or 500 words per hour if your homework is due sooner.

- Determine the number of days left on the homework and divide it into equal parts. For instance, five days means you have five equal parts on which to work.

- Math homework with 25 questions could easily be completed in an hour if each question were given two minutes.

How to Overcome Procrastination using Self Talk

We talk to ourselves all the time in our minds. Even when we're not paying attention, these relentless mental debates deeply influence our feelings and, ultimately, our behaviours and actions..

The good news is that if you can become aware of these mental dialogues, notice the patterns, and turn them into productive statements, then you are empowered to overcome many unwelcome feelings and behaviors.

Let's see how this can help us when it comes to procrastination.

Steps

1. Recognize the procrastinator's motto. Consider the following thought, which surely crosses our minds many times in one form or another:

"I have to finish this important task. It should already be done by now and I just need to do it."

This small, seemingly innocent thought contains almost every mental block that encourages procrastination. We all use the Procrastinator's Motto (or variations of it) every once in a while. If you're a chronic procrastinator, chances are you repeat it to yourself very frequently — daily, perhaps.

But what's so wrong about the Procrastinator's Motto? In what ways do these words encourage procrastination so much — and what can we do about it? Let's consider each part of this statement in turn, replacing each of them with an empowering alternative. In doing that, we'll turn the original motto on its head and create a productive call to action: a "Producer's Motto", if you like.

2. Remember that you don't 'have to' do anything. 'I have to' is every procrastinator's favorite expression. It's also the most disempowering. Every time you say to yourself that you *have to* do something, you imply that you don't have any choice, that you feel forced or coerced to do the task — that you don't really want to do it. That perception, of course, elicits a strong feeling of being victimized and resistance toward doing the task. The solution to this problem is to replace 'I have to' with the immensely more empowering alternative 'I choose to' or 'I will'. Everything you do is ultimately a choice (yes, even completing tax forms). Using language that expresses choice reminds you of that and brings the feeling of power back.

3. Focus on starting, rather than finishing. When you focus on finishing something, you direct your attention to a vague, highly idealized future. Visualizing a finished project is motivating for many people, but for someone who's having a hard time starting a task, visualizing a hard-to-grasp future can be overwhelming — even depressing. The solution in this case, then, is not to focus on finishing, but on starting. Forget for a minute about the finish line, just concentrate on giving your first step. Bring your focus from the future to what can be done right now. We all know that if we start something enough times, we'll eventually finish the task. Starting — all by itself — is usually sufficient to build enough momentum to keep the ball rolling.

4. Break a long project down into short tasks. Dwelling on the size and difficulty of a looming task will overwhelm us, and thus promote procrastination. Any undertaking, no matter how daunting, can be broken down into smaller steps. The trick is — with each step along the way — to focus solely on the next, achievable chunk of work. Ignore the big picture for a while and just tackle that next small task. Make sure you can easily visualize the outcome of your small task. Don't write a book; write a page. If it is still intimidating, commit yourself to work on it for a specific period of time. Keep the big picture in mind, of course, but don't allow it to frighten you. Use it for motivation and direction.

5. Don't place too much pressure on yourself. "This project has to impress everyone; I really can't blow this opportunity." Placing such high hopes on a project only adds anxiety and fear of failure. Perfectionism fuels procrastination. Overcome this mental block by simply giving yourself permission to be human. Allow yourself to be imperfect with the next small task. You can always refine your work later. If you're a serial perfectionist, go one step further and commit yourself to doing a sloppy job on purpose — at least at first. Instead of making every step perfect, think of them as steps *toward* perfection. For instance, write a page or two now, then proofread and correct them later.

6. Stop thinking about the way things 'should' be. The expression 'should' invokes blame and guilt. When you say you should be doing something (instead of what you're actually doing), you focus on comparing an ideal reality with your current, "bad" reality. You focus not on what is, but on what *could have been*. Misused 'shoulds' can elicit feelings of failure, depression and regret. The solution is not to focus on how you feel now, but on how good you *will feel* after you begin to take action.

7. Take some directed action. Even the tiniest progress is success — moving toward a goal is the best motivator. The trick is to bring that expected feeling of accomplishment into the present — and know that the real joy of progress is only a small task away. That small step is success.

Success is not the *end* of your task. Success is the *progress* that leads you to your next step.

8. Make it fun! "I've got to work all weekend". "I am trapped in this laborious project". Long periods of isolation can bring an enormous feeling of resentment. These feelings generate a strong sense of deprivation and resistance toward the task.

Overcome this mental block by avoiding long stretches of work. Schedule frequent and brief breaks. Plan small rewards along the way. One idea is to work near a break area. Have something to look forward to — not far away and not at the end of a long stretch — but in the very near future. When rewards are small, frequent, and *deserved*, they work wonders. Truly commit to brief bursts of relaxation and leisure time. In fact, go ahead and make it mandatory. This "reverse-psychology" can, by itself, give you a more productive and enjoyable mindset.

9. Rephrase your internal dialog. Time to check what we've accomplished with all the word substitutions. We started with:

"I have to finish this important task. It should already be done by now and I just need to do it."

And ended up with:

*"I choose to start this task with a **s**mall, imperfect step. I'll feel terrific and have plenty of time for fun!"* Quite a change, eh? Every time you catch yourself repeating any part of Procrastinator's Motto to yourself, stop and rephrase it. Then check how you feel. At first, it may seem to be a simple matter of word choices. But when you try this simple way of reframing your thoughts, you'll see how it instantly changes your attitude toward your tasks. Moreover, if you turn it into a habit, you'll slowly reprogram your thoughts, and make a positive, permanent change in your mindset.

CHAPTER 6 Improving Productivity

Productivity is very important for achieving goals on time. Techniques to improve productivity include avoiding procrastination, breaking down tasks for easier management and staying organized. Time management is best understood in confluence with the major topics that have been listed in the following chapter.

How to Overcome Laziness

Call it laziness, sloth, ineptitude, idleness, or whatever you like but the idea of doing nothing when things need to be done is often considered to be a sign of weakness or shirking. Sometimes laziness happens when you don't want to face something, like a boring chore or a difficult confrontation with someone. Other times, it might be because you feel overwhelmed and think the task needs a whole team rather than just you. And then there are those times where you really just can't be bothered. In any case. it's simply not a desirable trait.

Part 1

Setting Your Mind Straight

1. Figure out the real issue. Every time you start being lazy, stand back and do a little assessment of what's been really happening. Laziness is generally a symptom and not the problem itself. What's the cause of your lack of motivation? Are you tired, overwhelmed, afraid, hurting, or just plain uninspired and stuck? Most likely, the sticking issue is smaller than you think, and you can get past it more easily than you realize.

- Whatever it is that is holding you back, do your best to unearth it. In most cases, it'll be one single specific problem or detail. Finding the cause is the only way you can actually address it. Address it like you want it to happen. Once you address it, you can deal with it effectively.

2. Focus on the actual problem. Now that you're thinking about the cause of your laziness, start focusing on it. It may not be the quick fix you were looking for, but it'll be permanent. Consider the following:

- If you're tired, start devoting some time to relaxing. Everyone needs down time. If your schedule doesn't allow for it, you may have to make some sacrifices. But your output will be all the more better for it.

- If you're overwhelmed, take a step back. How can you simplify what's on your plate? Can you parse it into sections and make it smaller? Can you make a list of priorities and tackle them one at a time?

- If you're afraid, what are you afraid of? Obviously this is something you *wish* you were doing. Are you afraid of reaching your potential? Of finally hitting your goals and being unhappy? How can you see that your fear is irrational?

- If you're hurting, maybe the only answer is time. Grief, sadness, all those negative emotions won't go away at will. Our wounds need time to heal. Putting less pressure on yourself to stop hurting may be the catalyst for change you seek.

- If you're uninspired, what can you change about your routine? Can you put yourself in a different environment or is a mental demon you have to conquer? How can you vamp up everyday life? Think in terms of your senses. Music, food, sights, sounds, etc.

3. Get organized. Having clutter around us -- even when it's just visual -- can be a huge downer to our motivational skills. Whatever it is that could do for some organization, organize it. Whether it's your desk, your car, your whole house, or your routine, clean 'er up.

- There's a lot that's going on in our subconscious that we don't account for. Whether it's an unpleasant color palette or an inadequate amount of light or a lack of balance in some way, shape, or form, somewhere we know about it. Get rid of that tiny-but-powerful deterrent by getting organized.

4. Monitor that self-talk. Sometimes behaviors cause thoughts and sometimes thoughts cause behavior. Cover your bases and get rid of the negative inner dialogue. Thinking, "God, I'm so lazy. Ugh. Worthless," isn't going to get you anywhere. So stop it. Only you have control of that ticker tape going on behind your eyes.

- Every time you find yourself not performing up to par, twist it around to the positive. "It was a slow morning, but now it's time to fuel up. Now that it's afternoon, I'm buckling down!" You'll be surprised that the surge in mental positivity could actually change your outlook.

5. Practice mindfulness. So many of us don't take time to stop and smell the roses. We scarf down a great meal just to get to dessert, just to get to the wine, just to get to bed with an overly full stomach. We're always thinking about the next great thing instead of living in this wonderful moment that is right now. When we start living in the moment, we want to take advantage of it.

- Next time you find yourself thinking about the past or the future, draw yourself back into the present. Whether it's the scene around you, the food on your fork, or the music in your ears, let it show you how cool it is to be walking Earth and living. Sometimes stopping and slowing down can give us the energy to take advantage of what we have at our disposal.

6. Think of the benefits. Alright, so we got you focused on the present. Now let's focus on a better present. What would happen if you took advantage of right now? What would happen if instead of wasting away the morning in bed you got up and did yoga, finished your work, or cooked a great breakfast? What would happen if you did that practically every day for the next six months?

- It'd be wonderful, that's what. Let these positive ideas take over your train of thought. And be sure to realize that once you get going and develop the habit, everything will come that much easier.

Part 2

Getting Geared Up

1. Jump out of bed. Research tells us that hitting the snooze button is bad for us. You'd think lying there and enjoying the warmth of the covers would make you more energized later, but the opposite happens. We're actually more tired throughout the day. Instead, jump out of bed! Your mind will follow the cues your body is giving it. If you jump out of bed, you must be ready and raring to go.

- Literally jump if you can master it. Get your blood circulating. It may be the last thing you want to do, but if you can make yourself, you'll be all that more alive after.

2. Set some achievable goals. By setting yourself some worthy yet attainable goals, you have something to look forward to. Pick goals which really inspire you and that make the most of your talents and skills. Make a to-do list, both of large and small things, and prioritize each one in terms of time needed and importance to you personally.

- It may prove useful to keep a personal journal for each day of your target activities, with a record of what exactly may have helped or hindered you with regard to reaching your target as part of your practical logistics for self-development.

- Consider creating a vision board to post all your goals and dreams on. Be creative and use pictures, magazine articles, etc. Such a board can be used to fully map out your dreams. Each day upon waking, look at your vision board and focus on where you want to be. This will provide an inspired start to your day, and push you to your dreams.

  - Not everyone finds the vision board approach inspiring but there are other ways, such as mind maps, journals, creating a vision statement and telling others about it, making public pledges online to do something, etc.

3. Make a checklist of the desires, goals and motivations you want to move towards. As you power through them, check! Keeping the goals forefront in your mind requires actually focusing on them and a list can keep you energized through its ease of checking. Place copies of your goal sheet or routine everywhere: one on the fridge, on your night stand, by your computer, on your bathroom mirror, even on the bedroom door. Just place them where you look or go to often.

- Once those checks start accumulating, you won't want to stop. You'll literally see what you've been working towards and what you're capable of and that momentum will feel so good you'll have to keep going. You'd be disappointed and feel worse if you didn't.

4. Regularly revisit the importance and value of the problem or goal. Once you've settled on a goal or faced the problem in need of tackling, it doesn't miraculously direct you without effort on your behalf. Part of the success behind having a goal or finding a solution depends on reminding yourself of why it matters. If you lose sight of the goal or solution, it's easy to become embedded in distractions and dead-ends that make it seem too hard to continue, allowing laziness to set in. Regular reassessments of both the importance and value of the problem or goal will help to keep you focused and refreshed. Some things to ask yourself include:

- Is this something that I can actually afford to ignore or allow to go on unsolved for more time?

- Is this something that could be improved by having somebody else help me or share insights with me about?

- Am I using the right approach to solving this issue or pursuing this goal? (Sometimes it's time to follow a new approach than to keep pursuing the same old path.)

- Am I being perfectionist in my expectations? (Perfectionism can lead to procrastination, which can soon lead to nothing getting done because nothing is ever going to be good enough. The end result? Laziness sets in because it's "all too hard". Avoid falling into this vicious spiral by always doing your best, rather than focusing on aiming for nothing-but-perfection.)

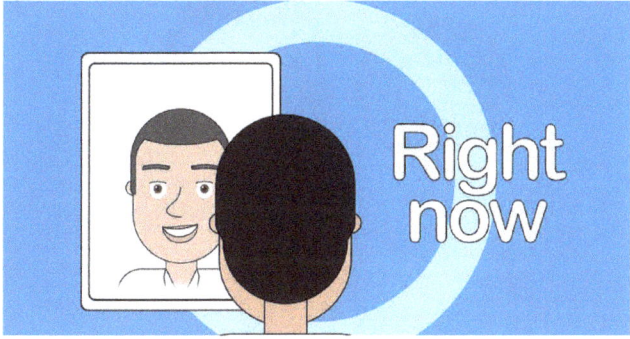

5. Tell yourself you ***can*** do something. Action changes everything. One moment you're passive and frozen; the next you're digging in and changing things simply because you moved, decided some-

thing or got out there. You are not defined by what went on before –– you are always in a position to reinvent yourself and make change happen. You just gotta think it and believe it.

- If you do feel stuck, try jumping up, doing the task, and telling yourself "Despite that old habit of freezing up, I am up *right now* and I *am* productive!" Keep your language in the present –– no conditional, future or past language should form part of your action statements. And definitely no "if only" statements –– those are for people who truly don't want to be fulfilled in life.

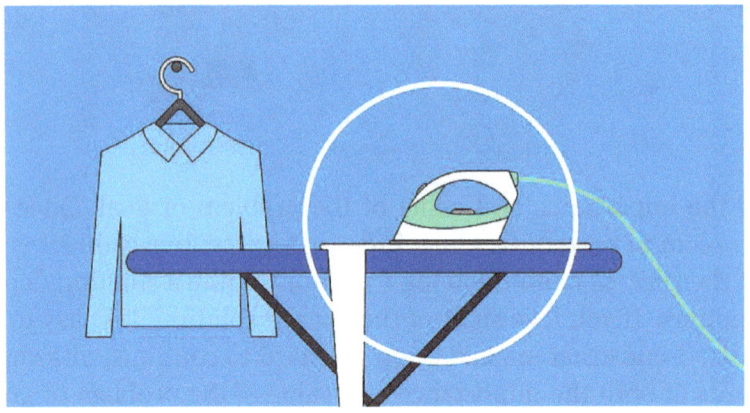

6. Iron your clothes. Let's say you're sitting on the couch, staring at your computer and all the would-be spreadsheets you wished would create themselves right now. Give it up. Instead, do something teeny, like ironing your clothes. You'll get out the iron, get out the board, get out your shirt, and five minutes into it you'll think, "Why am I wasting time ironing my clothes?" You'll put it down, be a little more awake from the activity, and get going on what you *actually* wanted to get done.

- And the other upside? You'll have a pressed shirt.

  - It doesn't have to be ironing, obviously. It could even be showering. Just getting up and doing something is sometimes the hardest obstacle -- when it's something small, it greases the tracks for us, making all activity smoother sailing.

7. Exercise. The benefits of exercise are innumerable, really, but one of the main ones is to feel more energized 24/7. It gets your blood flowing, your metabolism up, and your body in an ener-

gized state that lasts practically all day. If getting going in the morning is an issue for you, exercise for even 15 minutes. You'll feel more lively through the afternoon.

- Did we mention it's also a huge part of being healthy? When we're healthy, we feel better on the whole. If you're not currently exercising (especially aerobic, but anaerobic, too), make efforts to put it into your routine. The goal should be around 150 minutes a week, but whatever you can muster, do it.

- While we're at it, eat healthy, too. Junk food doesn't give your body the nutrients it needs to be active. A body lacking in energy can easily cause you to feel lazy and apathetic –– it's a good idea to get a doctor's check-up if you're worried about your nutrient intake or energy levels.

8. Dress the part. Sometimes we lack motivation for life. Just life. We become complacent in our jobs, our living situation, our relationships, and we just sort of fester in our own little world, knowing we should be trying harder to expand. The easiest way to start on that path to change? Dress differently.

- Whether you're a pizza delivery guy wishing you were on the floor of the Stock Exchange or a couch potato wishing you were running the Boston Marathon, changing your clothes may change your behavior. If you don't believe it, think of it this way: How would you address a guy in a suit? After a while, that guy in a suit starts living in a world that addresses him like a guy in a suit. So get your jogging pants on. Eventually you'll end up wondering why you're not jogging.

Part 3

Taking Action

1. Start. Everything begins somewhere, even if it's pulling the staples out of the piece of paper you have to get on with reading or wiping the fog off the windshield so you can drive the car out of your driveway. Overcoming the initial inertia that is natural for most human beings faced with difficult situations or tasks will immediately ease the pain of avoiding it. It will also highlight how to keep tackling it further. Eating the elephant one bite at a time will create momentum and you'll accumulate the confidence to stay motivated and find things less intimidating.

- Expecting life to be easy street is unrealistic –– life is often difficult, and sometimes, it's really difficult. But life is also wonderful, surprising, exciting and filled with hope. By being lazy, you excommunicate yourself from the possibilities of life and that's self-destructive. By improving your own attitude toward daily discomforts and learning to tolerate things that impact you, your resilience grows and you will find yourself becoming more constructive. Whenever something seems mammoth, hard and undesirable, just start it. Don't argue about it, don't make excuses, don't fight it––just get stuck into it with small steps.

2. Take your time. It's vital to break down your job into small steps. The smaller things are, the more accessible they are and the more doable they seem. When you actively seek a way to do a task or reach a goal that involves a sense of control and takes a relaxed approach, you'll feel capable rather than threatened. Often laziness is about feeling overwhelmed by everything and giving up because the mental hurdle before you seems too huge. The answer is to trust in the power of small.

- This doesn't mean you can't switch between tasks –– you most certainly can, and variety is the spice of maintaining interest. What it does mean though is that each small task must be done separately, with clean breaks between each one rather than fiddling here and there at the same time. Also, when moving between each task, find clean breakpoints so that it's easy to resume when you return to the task after a break.

- It is often said that those who complain they have no time are wasting it in inefficient ways, like multi-tasking. The human brain works inefficiently when there is constant pressure to do several things under tight deadlines –– in other words, multi-tasking dumbs us down. Free yourself by doing what matters in neat order, without guilt.

3. Give yourself pep talks. You are your own coach, your own source of inspiration. You can gear yourself into action by telling yourself inspiring things and affirming your actions. Tell yourself such things as: "I want to do this; I am doing this now!" and "I can take a break when this is done and that break will be deserved all the more for completing this task." Say these things out loud if needed. You'll feel motivated by giving voice to your actions.

- It may help to regularly recite an empowering mantra to yourself throughout the day, such as "I can do this, I know it." You can also visualize certain activities as already completed and anticipate the sense of accomplishment that you will experience when it's done.

4. Ask for help when you need it. Many people carry around an unwarranted fear that it's wrong to ask for the help of others. Whether this has developed as a result of an earlier unkind encounter, a stifling educational experience or a fiercely competitive workplace, it's an unhealthy attitude toward life. We are social beings and part of our existence is about sharing and helping one another.

Getting from "me to we" takes a little practice but it's an important part of growing and ceasing to struggle alone.

- Sometimes having another person hold us accountable is the impetus to action we need. If you're struggling with weight loss, get a workout buddy! That other person puts a pressure on us we can't put on ourselves (in a good way).

- Make sure to surround yourself with people that support and drive you. When all we know are draining relationships, it's easy to see why laziness is a problem. Find your inner circle of people that make you feel good and channel them for guidance.

5. Get real with yourself. Stay off the couch until you're ready to take a break. Even when you do sit, set a time when you'll return to your task or other activities such as reading a textbook, running a load of laundry or writing to a friend, etc. Self-discipline involves doing what you should do, when you should do it, whether you feel like it or not. No matter how early your training begins, this remains the most difficult lesson to master. Strike a healthy balance between being lenient and strict with yourself and prioritize business over pleasure.

- Rewards are sweetest when you have to wait for them and when they're deserved. You'll just end up being hard on yourself if you end up watching TV for two hours after 10 minutes of work. Resist. You'll feel better in the long run.

6. Compliment yourself every step of the way. Before you gulp at the possible arrogance of this, remember that this isn't a vanity-fest –– it's about maintaining your motivation. Whenever you finish a step, a small goal, a signpost along the way, find ways to cheer yourself on. Completing a task or effort will feel remarkably good each time.

- Celebrate the achievement by telling yourself that you've done well. Say something like: "Good stuff! You're on a roll; keep this up and you're going to make it to the end of this". Since big successes are made up of many little continuous successes (each small achievement is heroic), acknowledge your diligence accordingly.

Part 4

Staying Motivated

1. Learn to reward yourself for the very small things you complete or try. Occasional rewards will sweeten the tasks and help keep you on track. If you manage to do something that you didn't the day before or that you were absolutely dreading, you deserve a nice treat. By rewarding yourself after completion of small milestones along the way to the big one, you build in automatic reinforcement that you're doing the right thing. Keep most rewards simple but effective, such as extended breaks, catching a movie, splurging on a calorie-laden snack (once in a while!) or similar things. Leave really large rewards for the overall achievement or endpoint. By using self-rewards, you'll train your mind to actively seek working before the reward.

- Breaks are rewards *and* necessities. Don't confuse the need to take regular short breaks to restore creativity and freshness with laziness.

- Clearly, the flip side to rewards is punishment. People respond best to positive reinforcement and it's best to stick to the rewards. Punishing yourself for not achieving things will simply backfire, confirming your worst-held beliefs about yourself that you're lazy and good-for-nothing. That's a pointless exercise if ever there was one.

2. Write down your goals each week. A list of weekly goals will help you stay focused and motivated. As you go, it's inevitable that your goals will change. You'll also pinpoint the ways that are most effective for achieving them. As they morph, so should your list.

- Post the list everywhere and anywhere. Try making it your lock screen on your device or phone. To do this, simply write them in your notes, take a screenshot and make it your background. Create daily goals, monthly goals, and even yearly goals to keep looking at every day differently.

3. Realize that life is about trading costs and benefits. To enjoy any benefit, there is usually a cost to be suffered. The pain/suffering cost is usually emotional, often physical and sometimes psychic. Often that pain involves a feeling of being left out or going without while others don't seem to be putting up with the same challenges (usually they have their own challenges which you don't see though). And that pain can cause you to avoid, distract and seek safety in a comfort zone. To push past your comfort zone, you'll need to face the pain before you can reach the possibilities.

- Assess whether a potential benefit is worth the cost to you. If it is worth it (and most times, it will be), draw on your ever-evolving maturity to generate the required courage, endurance and discipline that will give you the strength to achieve brilliant outcomes. Nobody achieves anything without effort and pain.

4. Know that the work is worth it. Most experts, professionals and geniuses will readily admit that most of their achievements are 99 percent sweat and one percent talent. Undisciplined talent gets few people anywhere –– excellence in academics, financial autonomy, sports, the performing arts and relationships demands steady and consistent thoughtfulness and work that strains even the

best of us emotionally and physically. Your will to survive and flourish needs to translate to your will to work and suffer when to do so is both necessary and useful.

- You won't be a great businessman, a great runner, a great cook, or even great at your job overnight. You'll fail and fail and fail and fail. This is normal. This is good. This means you're still going.

5. Stay on track. There will be times when it gets harder and post-reward you can sometimes feel a bit flat about returning to the task at hand. In such times, you'll need to draw on inner reserves to remind yourself of the goal or solution sought to stay focused. Make the most of feeling that you're on a roll —– when you're in that state (often termed "the flow state"), use it to leap to another task or goal as soon as you're done rewarding yourself.

- The longer that you delay restarting after finishing one element in your tasks or goals, the harder it becomes to restart. Remember the feelings of being deeply involved in getting things done, and how good it feels to achieve things. And the sooner you restart, the more confident you'll feel and the sooner these good feelings will be restored.

6. Don't give up. It's one thing to find your motivation. But it's quite something else to keep it going when the going gets tough, especially in the face of unforeseen problems. Realize that interruptions happen, often for no reason, and they'll upend your efforts. Rather than letting setbacks demotivate you, see them for what they are and refuse to be flattened by them. You're not alone and staying focused on working through challenges is one of the best ways of coping and bouncing back.

- Remind yourself how much you want to achieve your goal or task, seek help where needed, take stock of what you have already achieved and then refuse to give up. You got this.

How to Prioritize

Sometimes it can start to seem like the whole world is crashing down. Work and school start piling up, house chores and responsibilities, commitments to friends and family--there just aren't enough hours in some days. Learning to prioritize effectively can help you become a more efficient worker, saving time, energy, and stress. Learn to organize your tasks into distinct categories and levels of difficult, and start approaching them like a pro. See Step 1 for more information.

Part 1

Making your to-do List

1. Choose a time-frame for your list. Do you have a particularly busy week coming up? A crazy day? Maybe thinking about everything you need to do before the end of the year is driving you nuts. Whatever the nature of your commitments, select the time-frame of the priorities list you hope to create to help you start managing those priorities and translating that stress into meaningful action.

- Short-Term Goals will often include things from many different categories. You might have several things you need to finish for work by the end of the day, as well as the errands you need to run before heading home, and various things to do around the house when you get there. You could have a list of stress-causers, all things that need to be done in the next several hours.

- Long-Term Goals might include larger ambitions that will need to be broken down into multiple steps you'll also need to prioritize. You might put "apply to colleges" on a long-term to-do list, which will involve many different smaller activities. The simple act of breaking it down, though, will simplify and demystify the process.

2. Write down everything you need to do. Start breaking it down and writing down what exactly you need to do in whatever order the things occur to you. Within the time frame that's got you stressing, select all the tasks--however big or small--that will need to be accomplished and list them out. List projects that need to be accomplished, decisions that need to be made, and errands that need to be run.

3. Categorize the things you need to do. It may be helpful to break everything up into separate categories, basically creating different to-do lists for the different areas of your life. House chores might be one category, while work projects or school projects may be another. If you've got a busy social life, there might be a lot going on during the weekend that you've also got to prepare for and prioritize. Create separate lists for each.

- Alternatively, if it helps you to have everything in one place, you might consider creating an over-all to-do of home chores and responsibilities, work commitments, and things necessary for your social life. If you're feeling overwhelmed, it can help to have everything juxtaposed with everything else, to let you start seeing the importance of individual tasks compared with others.

4. Put the list in order. Identify the most important or urgent activities on the list and rewrite the list with those at the top. It's all relative to you and the topics on your list, so you might decide that school activities trump work projects, or vice versa.

- Alternatively, if everything is equally important and necessary, keep the list unordered and approach it alphabetically or randomly. As long as you're actively ticking things off the list, all that matters is that you're getting things done.

5. Keep the list visible. Especially true for long-term lists, keep your list somewhere visible where you'll be able to use it as a reminder for what you need to finish, actively crossing out or checking off the items as you complete them.

- If you've got an analog list on a piece of paper, hang it somewhere you'll commonly look, like the refrigerator door or a bulletin board near the front door, or your office wall.

- Alternatively, you might keep a list on your desktop open while you work on other things, so you can keep it fresh in your mind and delete the items when you finish them.

- Post-it notes make for great around-the-house reminders. If you put a Post-it reminding you to work on your paper on the television screen, you'll remember to do what's important instead of wasting time doing something less productive.

Part 2

Ranking your Projects

1. Rank the importance of each task. What are the most important things on your list? In general, you might decide that work/school tasks will outweigh social and house-hold chores, though certain outliers may exist. You've got to eat and bathe, for example, though laundry might be able to wait another day while you finish an important work project.

- Decide on a few different levels, maybe three, to rank the different tasks and criteria on your list. High, medium, and low importance tasks might be the best and simplest way to start ranking the importance of things on your list. Be judicious in deciding.

2. Rank the urgency of each task. Consider upcoming deadlines and your ability to work within those deadlines. What needs to be done the soonest? What needs to be done by the end of the day? What might you be able to buy a bit more time on?

- It's important to consider the length of time it takes you to accomplish each of the tasks, maybe even assigning a set time to certain things. If you consider it a priority to exercise every day, but you've got a crazy amount of work to do, give yourself an exercise cap of 30 minutes and find somewhere to fit it in.

3. Rank the effort required for each task. It might be critical that you get something to post-office by the end of the day, but this isn't a terrifically difficult task. Rank everything on your list in terms of its difficult so you'll know how to situate it in relation to other tasks.

- It might be effective to use levels like Difficult, Moderate, and Easy to rank them, rather than trying to judge them in relation to one another. Don't worry about putting them in order before you've given each item its own rating, if it's helpful to do so.

4. Compare all the tasks and order the list. Put at the top of the list the most important and urgent tasks that will require the least amount of effort to try to maximize your work in the time you've allotted for it.

Part 3

Attacking the List

1. Do one thing at a time and see it through to completion. It's difficult to work your way through the list by cherry-picking and doing a little bit of everything. After several hours, your list will look just like it looks now: incomplete. Instead of working in little bits, do one thing until it's finished and then move to the next thing on your list after a short break. Don't work on something else on the list until you're finished with the first and most important things.

- Alternatively, you can look for projects from multiple lists that might be effectively combined. While it may not be a great idea to try to review your math notes and write your history paper at the same time, you might be able to sit at the laundromat and wait for your clothes to dry while studying, saving time getting important tasks finished.

2. Decide what to delegate and what to let slide. If the Internet is on the fritz at your house, it may be tempting to head to the library, start reading up on wi-fi so you can diagnose the problem from

scratch, but not if you've got to finish cooking dinner, grade twenty papers by the next morning, and do fifty other things. Might it be better to call the cable company instead?

- It's ok to decide something just isn't worth the time, or that delegating a task at a cost outweighs the time you might spend on it. You could buy new expensive fence wire, or you could salvage your own by combing through the junkyard painstakingly, sifting through rough scrap for several hours in the hot sun, but if it only turns out to be a few bucks of savings, it might be more worth it to buy new wire.

3. Alternate the variety of tasks on your list. Breaking up the sorts of activities you do will help keep you fresh throughout your tasks and help you move through your list more quickly. Alternate a homework list with a housework list to be the most effective worker you can be. Take short breaks between them and do different tasks. You'll stay fresh and efficient.

4. Start with the least desirable or the hardest tasks. Depending on your temperament, it can be good for your own morale if you accomplish the thing first that you're looking forward to the least. It might not necessarily be the hardest or the most important thing, but getting it out of the way to save the less painful activities for later could be effective for some people.

- Your English essay might be more important than your math homework, but if you really hate math, get it out of the way first so you can clear out all the time you need to devote solely to the essay, giving it your full, unfettered attention.

5. Let importance trump urgency in some cases. You might have a situation in which you've only got 10 minutes to get all the way across town to the library to pick up the new disc of Game of Thrones you ordered, making it the most urgent thing on your list, but that time might be better spent doing the more-important task of getting to work on your English essay. You'll have bought yourself more time by waiting to pick up your DVD until the next day, when you might have more time for it.

6. Cross tasks off the list as you complete them. Congratulations! As you move through the list, take a glad moment to cross each thing off, deleting it from the file, or aggressively cutting it off the paper with a rusty pocketknife and ceremonially setting the scrap on fire. Take a minute to reward yourself for each little accomplishment. You're doing it!

How to be More Productive

Everyone would like to be able to accomplish more in less time. It is easy to just accept that some people are naturally more productive and others more prone to procrastination. However true that may be, it is also clear that productive people take advantage of various useful strategies that can benefit anyone.

Method 1

Getting Organized

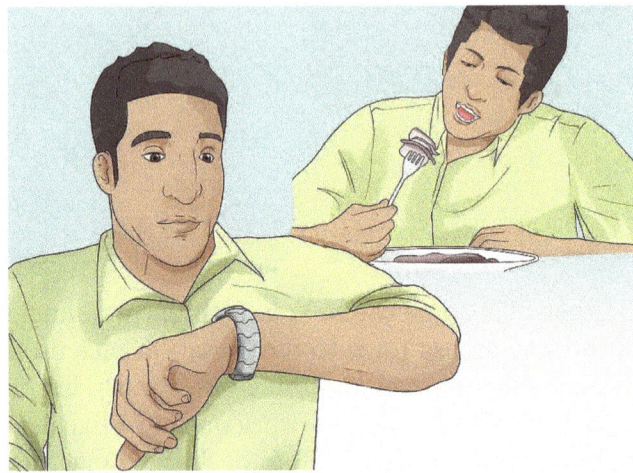

1. Set a routine. Plot out recurring times in your schedule when you can focus your energies on the specific tasks you need to accomplish. Incorporate them into you existing daily routines (getting ready for work, lunchtime, etc.). Just as your body tells you "this is lunchtime" around the time you normally eat, you will become more attuned to feeling that "this is productive time."

2. Break up larger tasks. Don't focus on needing to write the entire book or paint the whole house; focus on finishing a chapter or a room. The sense of accomplishment will help keep you going, and it provides a way to mark your progress towards the larger goal.

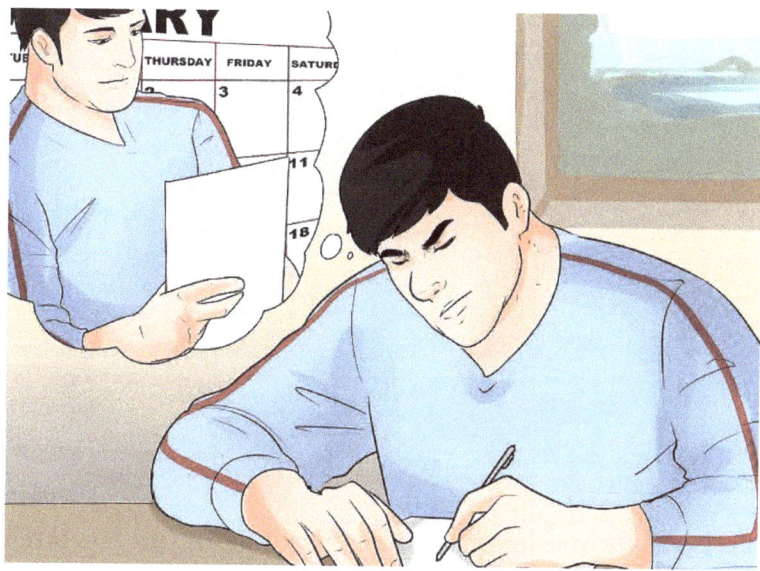

3. Create deadlines. Remember that time you had to finish a college term paper in one night? When there is a clear time limit, you have no choice but to focus your energies and stick to the essentials of your goal.

- If you're already on a deadline, set up mini-deadlines for components of the task.

- Try to be strict with yourself as it is easy to break self-created deadlines. Put your deadline up against an appointment you can't miss or just set an egg timer.

4. Establish the right amount of time to finish the job. "Work expands to fill the time" -- what sounds like old-fashioned wisdom can also be expressed by mathematical formulas, but the point of Parkinson's Law remains the same. Basically, if you give yourself all day to accomplish a task, you'll find a way to take all day to do it (or overdo it, that is). Figure out the minimum amount of time you need to do the job up to the necessary standard.

5. Plan but be flexible. Do all the routine-making and deadline-setting you can, but also realize that life will intervene and you will need to be able to adjust. Don't let disruptions throw you completely off your rhythm. See if you can find ways to take advantage of them, or at least brush them off.

- For example, if you're trying to finish up a presentation for tomorrow morning and the power goes out, recruit someone to help you practice the Q&A session that follows until power is restored. Or even use it to make a lame joke the next day about how a competitor tried to sabotage your clearly blackout-proof presentation.

Method 2

Listening to your Body

1. Know oneself. If you're a morning person or a "night owl," take advantage of that. Maximize your most productive times. If music helps you focus, use it; if it distracts you, forget it.

- Think about what has worked when you've been productive in the past. Did your college finals studying go better when you holed up in a silent corner of the library or when your room-mates were playing video games three feet away?

2. Take "mindless breaks." When your brain is fried and you need to step away, do it. Watch a soap opera, walk your dog, clean a few of those dusty shelves you've been meaning to get to.

- Expect to need such breaks and factor them into your schedule. This way you won't feel like you're wasting time while you're, well, wasting time (but in a positive way).

3. Get out in the sun. Natural sunlight helps keep your body rhythms balanced, gives you energy, and just plain feels good. Take a walk or work by a window when you can.

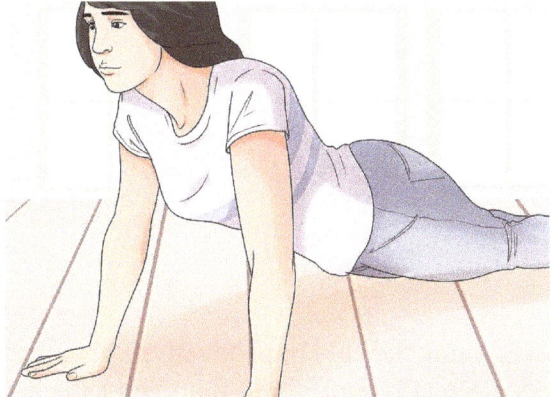

4. Exercise. It breaks up the monotony of the day, relieves stress, helps you refocus your mind, and it's good for you.

5. Do a "brain dump." As you work on a project, your mind will fill up with ideas, some relevant to the current task, some not. If you're feeling bogged down or stuck as you try to figure out a task, work on emptying your mind of distracting ideas. But keep them around just in case!

- Jot down your scattered ideas in a notepad (or your preferred more technologically advanced device) at the end of the day or when you're feeling mentally overloaded.

- Don't worry about connecting all the dots right now. This is another form of brainstorming; get the ideas out, figure out what works, what doesn't, and how they connect later.

Method 3

Prioritizing

1. Be realistic. Some people who think they are unproductive are in fact productive people who just expect too much of themselves. Don't bite off more than you can chew. Productive people aren't 'super-humans'; they know what they can accomplish (and their limits) and focus on getting the job done.

- Consider whether you would ask someone else to accomplish as much as you're attempting. If you would feel bad asking someone else to do that much, you're probably asking too much of yourself.

- At the end of the day, write down a list of all that you did accomplish. It might surprise you, and it will give you something else to look at other than that lengthy to-do list you started with that morning.

2. Keep it simple. Think about the essential element(s) of what it is you want or need to accomplish. It is easier to hit a clear target.

- Focus on your results, not on the time it takes to get there. After all, we're usually judged on results. We don't care how long it took the baker to make our wedding cake or what methods he used; we just want it to look and taste great.

3. Determine the importance and urgency of your tasks. Like a good general (and pretty decent President) should, Dwight Eisenhower knew how to get things done. He made a point of determin-

ing what was truly important and truly urgent, and was known to say "What is important is seldom urgent, and what is urgent is seldom important."

- The Eisenhower Box breaks tasks into four categories: Important and Urgent (do those now); Important but Not Urgent (decide when you want to do those later); Not Important but Urgent (delegate those to others); Not Important and Not Urgent (delete those from your list).

- Of course, not everyone has the same ability to delegate tasks as does a general or President, but such tasks can also be opportunities for collaborative work. Know your strengths, and the strengths of those around you.

4. Know what is most important. We all want to be more productive, but if your quest for productivity is severely curtailing you family time or damaging something else of great value to you, take a step back and prioritize your values. If you gain exceptional productivity at the cost of something far more precious to you, what have you truly gained?

How to Create an Effective Action Plan

Creating a powerful action plan always begins with having a clear purpose, vision or goal in mind. It is designed to take you from wherever you are right now directly to the accomplishment of your stated goal. With a well-designed plan, you can achieve virtually any goal you set out to accomplish.

Part 1

Creating Your Plan

1. Keep a record of everything. As you work through your action plan, keep notes of everything. You may find it helpful to have a binder with different tabs in it to section off different aspects of your planning process. Some examples of sections:

- Ideas/Miscellaneous notes

- Daily Schedules

- Monthly Schedules

- Milestones

- Research

- Follow-up

- Individuals involved/Contacts

2. Know what you want to do. The less clear you are about what you want to do, the less effective your plan will be. Try to specifically define what you want to achieve as early as possible — preferably before starting your project.

- Example: You are trying to complete your master's thesis — basically a very long essay — which needs to be about 40,000 words. It will include an introduction, a literature review (in which you critically discuss other research that informs yours, and discuss your methodology), several chapters in which you put your ideas into practise using concrete examples, and a conclusion. You have 1 year to write it.

3. Be specific and realistic in your planning. Having a specific goal is just the beginning: you need to be specific and realistic in every aspect of your project — for example, by stating specific and achievable schedules, milestones, and final outcomes.

- Being specific and realistic while planning a long project is all about pro-actively reducing stress that can accompany poorly planned projects such as missed deadlines and exhausting long hours.

- Example: To finish your thesis on time, you need to write roughly 5,000 words per month, which will give you a couple of months at the end of your timeline to polish your ideas. Being realistic means not placing the expectation on yourself to write more than 5,000 words each month.

- If you're working as a teaching assistant for three of those months, you'll need to consider that you may not be able to complete 15,000 words in that time, and you'll need to spread that amount out over your other months.

4. Set measurable milestones. Milestones mark significant stages along the road to achieving your end goal. Create milestones easily by starting at the end (the accomplishment of the goal) and working your way backwards to your present day and circumstances.

- Having milestones can help you — and if applicable, your team — stay motivated by breaking the work into smaller chunks and tangible goals so that you don't need to wait until the project is completely finished to feel as though you've accomplished something.

- Don't leave too much time or too little time between milestones — spacing them two weeks apart has been found to be effective.

- Example: When writing your thesis, resist the urge to set milestones based on chapter completions, as this could be a matter of months. Instead, set smaller milestones — perhaps based on word counts — every two weeks, and reward yourself when you hit them.

5. Break large tasks into smaller, more manageable chunks. Some tasks or milestones may seem more daunting to achieve than others.

- If you're feeling overwhelmed by a large task, you can help ease your anxiety and make it feel more doable by breaking it down into smaller, more manageable chunks.

- Example: The lit review is often the most difficult chapter to write, as it forms the foundation of your thesis. In order to complete your lit review, you need to do a significant amount of research and analysis before you can even begin writing.

- You can break it into three smaller chunks: research, analysis, and writing. You can break it down even smaller by choosing specific articles and books that you need to read, and setting deadlines for analyzing them and writing about them.

6. Make scheduled lists. Make a list of tasks that you need to complete in order to hit your milestones. A list on its own will not be effective — you must write this list into a timeline associated with specific, realistic actions.

- Example: By breaking your lit review into smaller chunks, you'll know exactly what you need to get done, and can figure out a realistic timeframe for those tasks. Perhaps every one to two days you will have to read, analyze, and write about one key reading.

7. Put timelines on everything. Without specific time frames and deadlines, work will definitely expand to fill the time allotted, and some tasks may never get completed.

- No matter what action items you choose for which phase of your action plan, it is essential that a time frame be attached to absolutely everything.

- Example: If you know that it takes you roughly 1 hour to read 2,000 words, and you'll be reading a 10,000-word article, you need to give yourself at least 5 hours to complete that article.

- You'll need to also account for at least 2 meals during that time, as well as short breaks every 1 to 2 hours for when your brain is feeling tired. In addition, you'll want to add at least an hour onto your final number just to account for any possible unanticipated interruptions.

8. Create a visual representation. Once you've listed your action items and set a specific timeline, the next step is to create some type of visual representation of your plan. You might use a flow chart, a Gantt chart, a spreadsheet, or some other type of business tool to accomplish this.

- Keep this visual representation in an easily accessible place — even on a wall in your office or study room, if possible.

9. Mark things off as you go. Marking things off as you go will not only feel satisfying, it will help you keep on track lest you forget what you've already done.

- This is particularly important if you're working with other people. If you're working with other people, you might consider using a shared online document so that everyone can check in no matter where they are.

10. Don't stop until you've reached your final goal. Once your plan is established and shared with the team (if applicable), and your milestones are scheduled, the next step is simple: take daily actions to achieve your goal.

11. Change the date if you must, but never give up on your goal. Occasionally, circumstances or unforeseen events can arise that throw a wrench in your ability to meet deadlines, complete tasks and achieve your goal.

- If this happens, do not get discouraged – revise your plan and continue working to meet targets and move forward.

Part 2

Managing your Time

1. Get yourself a good planner. Whether this is an app or a book, you'll need a planner that will allow you to plan out your time by the hour, each day of the week. Make sure it's easy to read and easy to use, otherwise you'll likely not make use of it.

- Studies have shown that physically writing things down (i.e. with pen and paper) will make you more likely to do them. For this reason, you may be best off using a physical planner to plan your time out.

2. Avoid to-do lists. So you have a long list of things to do, but when will you actually do them? To-do lists are not as effective as scheduling out your tasks. When you schedule your tasks, you make the time to get them done.

- When you have specific time blocks in which to work (many day planners literally contain hourly time blocks), you'll also find that you're less likely to procrastinate, as you only have an allotted time in which to get your work done before you must move on to the next scheduled task.

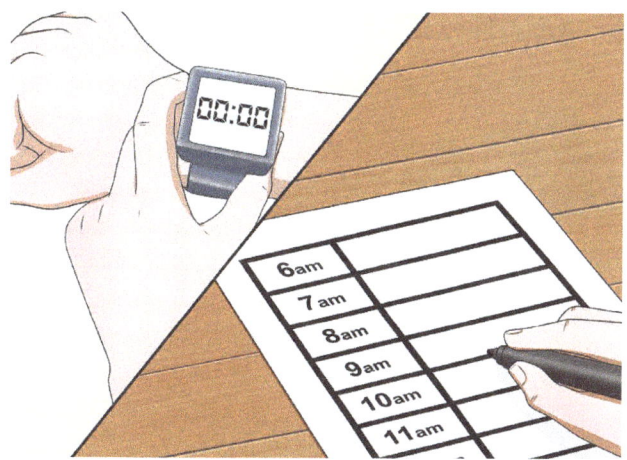

3. Learn how to time block. Blocking out your time helps you get a more realistic idea of how much time you actually have in a day. Start with your highest-priority tasks and work backwards.

- Do this for your whole week. Having a broader view of how your days will add up will help you refine your schedule to be as productive as possible.

- Some experts even suggest having at least a general idea of what your whole month will look like.

- Some people recommend starting at the end of your day and working backwards — so if you're done work/homework at 5 p.m., plan backwards from there, to when your day starts, for example, at 7 a.m.

4. Schedule time for leisure and breaks. Studies have shown that scheduling even your free time can help increase your satisfaction with life. It has also been proven that long work hours (50+ hours a week) in fact make you less productive.

- Sleep deprivation will kill your productivity. Make sure that you sleep at least 7 hours each night if you're an adult, or 8.5 hours a night if you're a teenager.

- Studies show that scheduling small, "strategic renewals" (i.e. workouts, brief naps, meditation, stretching) into your day will boost your productivity and overall health.

5. Set aside time to plan your week out. Many experts suggest scheduling time right at the start of your week to sit down and plan your week. Figure out how you can best use each day to work toward achieving your goals.

- Account for any work or social obligations you have; if you find your schedule is tight, you may need to drop some of your lower-priority plans.

- This doesn't mean dropping social activities. It's important to keep up with your good friends and to nurture your close relationships. You need a support network.

6. Know what a sample scheduled day looks like. To return to the thesis-writing example, a regular day might look something like this:

- 7 a.m.: Wake up

- 7:15 a.m.: Exercise

- 8:30 a.m.: Shower and dress

- 9:15 a.m.: Make and eat breakfast

- 10 a.m.: Work on Thesis - writing (plus 15 minutes of small breaks)

- 12:15 p.m.: Lunch

- 1:15 p.m.: Emails

- 2 p.m.: Research and response to research (including 20 to 30 minutes of breaks/snacks)

- 5 p.m.: Wrap up, check emails, set primary goals for tomorrow

- 5:45 p.m.: Leave desk, go grocery shopping

- 7:00 p.m.: Make dinner, eat

- 9:00 p.m.: Relax — play music

- 10:00 p.m.: Prepare for bed, read in bed (30 minutes), sleep

MONDAY	TUESDAY	WEDNESDAY	THURSDAY	FRIDAY
Writing research	Learning musical instrument	Writing research	Learning musical instrument	Writing research

7. Know that every day does not have to look the same. You can split up tasks into only 1 or 2 days a week — sometimes it's even helpful to break up tasks as you can return to them with a fresh perspective.

- Example: Maybe you only write and do research Mondays, Wednesdays, and Fridays, and on Thursdays you substitute writing with learning a musical instrument.

8. Schedule for problems. Build a little bit of extra time into every block that will account for a slow work day or an unanticipated interruption. A good rule of thumb is to give yourself double the time you expect a task to take — particularly when you're just starting out.

- As you become more comfortable with your tasks, or if you already have a good sense of how long something will take, you can shave your time down, but it's always a good idea to leave in at least a small buffer.

9. Be flexible and gentle with yourself. Especially as you're starting out, be prepared to tweak your schedule as you go. It's part of the learning process. You may find it helpful to block your time out in pencil.

- You may also find it helpful to spend a week or two recording what you do each day into a planner as you go. This will help you get a sense of how you spend your time and how much time each task takes.

10. Disconnect. Set times in your day where you'll check your emails or social media. Be strict with yourself, as it's possible to lose hours just checking in every few minutes here and there.

- This includes turning off your phone, if possible — at least for periods where you really want to focus on work.

11. Do less. This relates to disconnecting. Figure out the most important things in your day — the ones that will help you achieve your goals, and focus on those. De-prioritize the less important things that fragment your day: emails, mindless paperwork, etc.

- One expert recommends not checking your emails for at least the first one or two hours of your day; this way, you can focus on your important tasks without getting distracted by the things that those emails may contain.

- If you know you have a lot of small tasks to do (for example, email, paperwork, tidying up your workspace), group them together into a chunk of time in your schedule rather than allowing them to fragment your day or break the flow of other more important tasks that might require more concentration.

Part 3

Staying Motivated

1. Be positive. Staying positive is fundamental to achieving your goals. Believe in yourself and the people around you. Counter any negative self-talk with positive affirmations.

- In addition to being positive, you will benefit from surrounding yourself with positive people. Research has shown that over time, you adopt the habits of those with whom you spend the most time, so choose your company wisely.

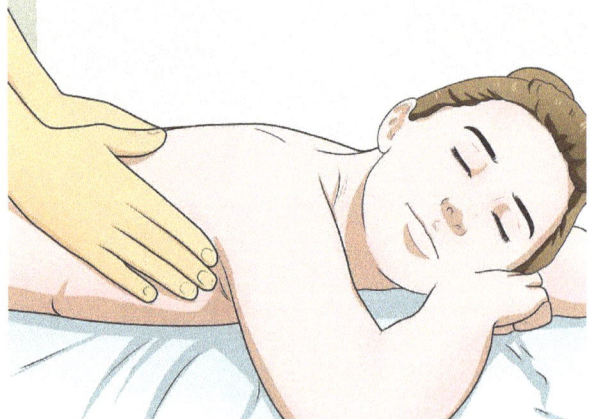

2. Reward yourself. This is particularly important to do each time you hit a milestone. Give yourself tangible rewards — for example, a nice dinner at your favorite restaurant when you hit your first two-week milestone, or a back massage for your two-month milestone.

- One expert suggests giving a friend money and telling them that they can only give it to you if you finish a given task by a specified time. If you don't finish the task, your friend keeps the money.

3. Get a support network. It's important to have your friends and family on your side; it's also important to build connections with people who have similar goals to you. That way you can check in with each other.

4. Track your progress. Research has shown that progress is the highest motivator. You can track your progress simply by ticking off tasks in your schedule as you go.

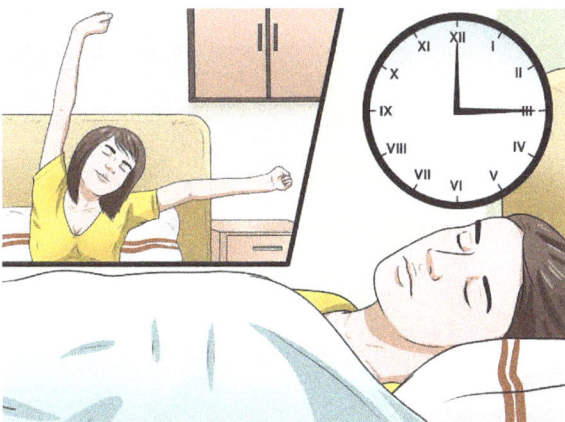

5. Go to bed early and get up early. When you read about the schedules of highly productive people, a large percentage of them start their days early. These people also have a morning routine — often this is something they can look forward to doing before they go to work.

- Positive ways to start the morning are to do some sort of exercise (from light stretching and yoga to an hour at the gym), eat a healthy breakfast, and spend 20 to 30 minutes writing in a journal.

6. Give yourself downtime. Taking breaks is imperative to staying motivated. If you are always working, you'll wind up exhausting yourself. Taking breaks is a pro-active way to prevent yourself from getting exhausted and losing time that you don't want to lose.

- Example: Step away from your computer, turn off your phone, just sit somewhere quiet and do nothing. If ideas come to you, write them down in a notebook; if they don't, enjoy having nothing to do.

- Example: Meditate. Turn off your phone's ringer, turn off any notifications that you might get, and set a timer for up to 30 minutes, or however long you can afford. Just sit quietly and try to clear your mind. When thoughts come into your mind, you might find it useful to label them and then let them go — for example, if you think about work, just quietly say in your head, "Work" and then let it go, and keep doing this as the thoughts arise.

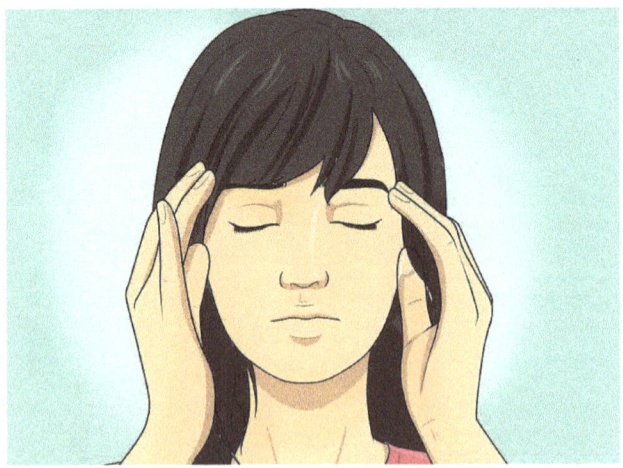

7. Visualize. Take a few minutes now and then to think about your goal and how it will feel to have achieved it. This will help you get through the harder times that may accompany pursuing your goal.

8. Know that it won't be easy. Things worth having are rarely easy to get. You may have to resolve a lot of issues or work through some things as you work toward your goal. Accept them as they come.

- Many gurus who extol the virtue of living in the present advise to accept setbacks as though you chose them yourself. Instead of fighting them or getting upset, accept them, learn from them, and set to work figuring out how you'll achieve your goal given the changed circumstances.

Part 4

Identifying your Goals

1. Write about what you want. Do this in a journal or a text document. This is particularly helpful if you're not entirely sure what you want to do, but just have a feeling about it.

- Writing regularly in a journal is a great way to keep in touch with yourself and to keep up to date on how you're feeling. Many people claim that writing helps them clarify how they feel and what they want.

2. Do your research. Once you have an idea of what you want to do, do your research. Researching your goals will help you narrow down the best way to achieve them.

- Online forums like Reddit are a great place to look for discussions on most topics — particularly if you want an insider's view on specific careers.

- Example: While writing your thesis you're beginning to wonder what you'll end up doing with it. Read about what others have done with similar degrees to the one that you're pursuing. This might even help you gear your thesis towards publications or other opportunities that can help further your career.

3. Consider your options and choose the one that best serves you. After you've done your research you'll have a good sense of what each path and result will look like. This should make it easier for you to choose the path that will best serve you in achieving your goal.

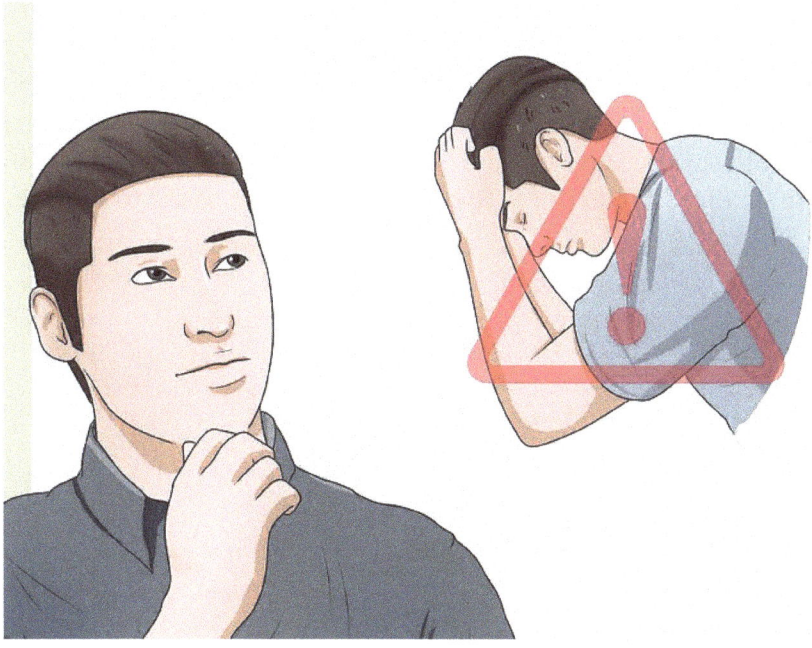

4. Be aware of things related to your goal that may affect you. This includes being aware of things that may hinder you in your goals — in the case of thesis writing this may include mental exhaustion, lack of research, or unexpected work responsibilities.

5. Be flexible. Your goals may change as you move toward them. Allow room for yourself, and as a result, your goals, to develop. That said, don't just give up when it gets hard. There's a difference between losing interest and losing hope!

How to Make Large Tasks Small

Are you someone who get overwhelmed by large tasks? Do you have trouble managing time? Are your grades or work suffering because of this? What this article teaches you is how to take huge tasks and then create smaller simpler ones. These goals are much easier to achieve.

Steps

1. First look at your task and ask yourself, "What is it that I'm trying to accomplish?" This may seem stupid but in the long run this can help you to create a plan to accomplish your task.

2. Set a specific achievable goal. For example, let's say you want to get higher grades. Ask yourself what type of grades do you want. Let's say your goal is have a 90 GPA in the next marking period.

3. Take this large task and break it down into smaller ones. In this case take this task one test at a time.

4. Work to achieve each smaller task. By studying for that one test over a weeks time, you should get a very high grade, but like any high school student you don't just have one test.

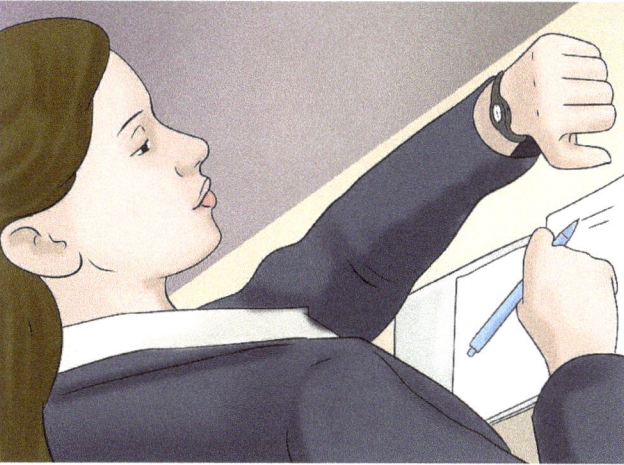

5. Manage your time. Study for the test from when you find out about the test(s) to the day before the test(s)this will let you study for multiple tests without causing too much stress.

6. Weekends should be used to relax as well as study. Set a time for study and time for play. Perhaps you like to do your homework/ studying in the morning. This lets you enjoy your weekend while also getting work done.

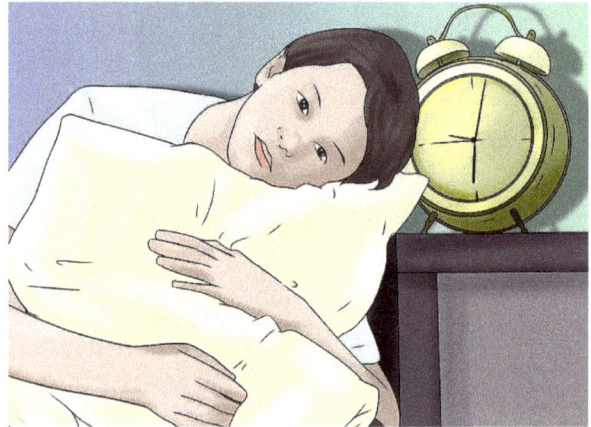

7. Focus on your overall goal and bounce back. If you don't do well on one test, don't get saddened. Try to do better on the next test.

8. Finally concentrate. If you lack discipline this might be a hard task. Never give up and try to remember your original goal.

7 Time Allocation and Time Tracking Software

Time allocation is an important aspect in achieving goals. Working under a deadline requires strict allocation of time for completion of tasks. Techniques and software available that can evaluate the time spent on tasks are explained in this chapter.

Time Allocation

Time management

Time allocation is the allotment of time that has been used within different activities and specific exercises. Time allocation can measure how natural and effective the human behaviour is towards completing tasks and activities within a particular time frame. this can be used to also find out how much time an individual is spending on a specific task, for where they can then try to improve their timing by using various improvement and tactical methods. This will then hopefully lead to an sharp increase in productivity and a certain satisfaction for the particular individual, as they will soon realise they have more time do other necessary tasks and commitments.

One vital factor in successful time allocation is the decision of where to use the right amount of time. In order to shine in one particular task, one must allocate more time to it, which will result in allocating less time to another specific task.

How To Allocate Time Effectively and Efficiently

Decide Where you will not Spend Time

Keeping in mind that you only have a limited time budget, you may not have the time and ability to do everything you would like to complete - not including your efficiency levels. Once you actually realise that, you instantly feel more calm, as you now tend to believe that the particular task can either be delayed/ postponed or even carried/delegated to someone else that you choose. For example, if an individual wanted to finish off some home decor, they can hire specialists to finish off the job whilst that particular individual can carry on doing something more important such as calculating the costs of doing up his/her house.

Strategically Allocate your Time

Strategically allocating your precious time into work and your own personal life can really help to ensure that individuals have the proper investment in each task and activity that they may need to carry out. The consequence of focusing more time on specific set tasks reduces the overall amount of time that you could've possibly had in doing something more beneficial. Such as working extremely long hours in one particular task during the day may leave you with insufficient funds for activities like exercise, sleep, and relationships, to make up for during the rest of the remaining day.

Aim for a Consistently Balanced Time Budget

Time allocation

In every day life, you will have unexpected circumstances occurring, which will disrupt a potential desired balanced time budget. For example, you can't expect that you will have a constantly balanced time budget every single day or week, however, you can aim for consistency. Over the course of a one to two week period, your time investment should reflect your priorities, which will therefore clearly show what tasks you are naturally likely to prioritise over others.

Cost and Benefits of Time Allocation Research Methods

Methods of Direct Observations (Spot-checks)

The spot-check method uses a random pattern of "checks" to determine what the participants of the study population are doing at a specific time. By randomly selecting the observations by person and time, a representative sample, allows a statistically and relatively accurate picture of patterns of time.

Methods Depending on Self Support

A potential increase in accuracy is achieved by asking informants to report their activities over the previous 24-hour period. Informants can generally remember bedtimes, mealtimes, and the estimated times spent in lengthy activities such as going to work or even playing sports like Football or Rugby. By careful assessing, an interviewer can help the individual retain information and data from the previous day in extreme detail, retrieving smaller pieces of behaviour.

Methods Depending on Self Support

In this particular method, individuals are asked to keep records of their own daily tasks and activities. The reliability of the data can differ between being very high or very low, due to the fact that it is entirely reliable on how well-prepared the informants are, and how committed to the research goals they wish to follow. Without a doubt, if they view the task with boredom, the results will be low; but if they can be motivated to keep detailed records of their activities at certain intervals during their day, this method can prove to be very beneficial and effective.

Timeboxing

In time management, timeboxing allocates a fixed time period, called a time box, to each planned activity. Several project management approaches use timeboxing. It is also used for individual use to address personal tasks in a smaller time frame. It often involves having deliverables and deadlines, which will improve the productivity of the user.

> 66   99
>
> Timebox—don't scopebox.

— *Mary Poppendieck , Leading Lean*
Software Development—

In Project Management

Timeboxing is used as a project planning technique. The schedule is divided into a number of separate time periods (timeboxes), with each part having its own deliverables, deadline and budget.

As An Alternative to Fixing Scope

In project management, the triple constraints are time (sometimes schedule), cost (sometimes budget), and scope (sometimes performance). Quality is often added, sometimes replacing cost. Changing one constraint will probably impact the rest.

Without timeboxing, projects usually work to a fixed scope, such that when it is clear that some deliverables cannot be completed, either the deadline slips (to allow more time) or more people are involved (to do more in the same time). Usually both happen, delivery is late, costs go up, and often quality suffers (as per the The Mythical Man-Month principle).

With timeboxing, the deadline is fixed, but the scope may be reduced. This focuses work on the most important deliverables. For this reason, timeboxing depends on the prioritisation (with the MoSCoW method for example) of deliverables, to ensure that it is the project stakeholders who determine the important deliverables rather than software developers.

To Manage Risk

Timeboxes are used as a form of risk management, to explicitly identify uncertain task/time relationships, i.e., work that may easily extend past its deadline. Time constraints are often a primary driver in planning and should not be changed without considering project or sub-project critical paths. That is, it's usually important to meet deadlines. Risk factors for missed deadlines can include complications upstream of the project, planning errors within the project, team-related issues, or faulty execution of the plan. Upstream issues might include changes in project mission or backing/support from management. A common planning error is inadequate task breakdown, which can lead to underestimation of the time required to perform the work. Team-related issues can include trouble with inter-team communication; lack of experience or required cross-functionality; lack of commitment/drive/motivation (i.e. poor team building and management).

To stay on deadline, the following actions against the triple constraints are commonly evaluated:

- Reduce scope: drop requirements of lower impact (the ones that will not be directly missed by the user)

- Time is the fixed constraint here

- Increase cost: e.g., add overtime or resources

Adoption in Software Development

Many successful software development projects use timeboxing, especially smaller ones. Adopting timeboxing more than tripled developer productivity at DuPont in the '80s. In some cases, applications were completely delivered within the time estimated to complete just a specification. However, Steve McConnell argues that not every product is suitable and that timeboxing should only be used after the customer agrees to cut features, not quality. There is little evidence for strong adoption amongst the largest class of projects.

Timeboxing has been adopted by some notable software development methodologies:

- Dynamic systems development method (DSDM)

- In lean software development, pull scheduling with Kanban provides short term time management. When developing a large and complex system, when long term planning is required timeboxing is layered above.

- Rapid application development (RAD) software development process features iterative development and software prototyping. According to Steve McConnell, timeboxing is a "Best Practice" for RAD and a typical timebox length should be 60–120 days.

- Scrum was influenced by ideas of timeboxing and iterative development. Regular timeboxed units known as sprints form the basic unit of development. A typical length for a sprint is 30 days. Sprint planning, sprint retrospective and sprint review meetings are timeboxed.

- In Extreme programming methodologies, development planning is timeboxed into iterations typically 1, 2 or 3 weeks in length. The business revalues pending user stories before each iteration.

Agile software development advocates moving from plan driven to value driven development. Quality and time are fixed but flexibility allowed in scope. Delivering the most important features first leads to an earlier return on investment than the waterfall model.

A lack of detailed specifications typically is the result of a lack of time, or the lack of knowledge of the desired end result (solution). In many types of projects, and especially in software engineering, analyzing and defining all requirements and specifications before the start of the realization phase is impossible. Timeboxing can be a favorable type of contracting for projects in which the deadline is the most critical aspect and when not all requirements are completely specified up front.

This is also a better structure for allowing for new insights that are developed during the project to be reflected in the end result.

In Personal Time Management

Individuals can use timeboxing for personal tasks, as well. This technique utilizes a reduced scale of time (e.g., thirty minutes instead of a week) and deliverables (e.g., chores instead of a component of a business project). Personal timeboxing is said to help curb perfectionist tendencies (by setting a firm time and not overcommitting to a task). It is also suggested that personal time boxing can create an increased pressure for an individual which will lead to better creativity and focus towards a task.

Relationship with Other Methods

Timeboxing acts as a building block in other personal time management methods:

- The Pomodoro Technique is based on 25 minute timeboxes of focused concentration separated by breaks allowing the mind to recover.

- Andy Hunt gives timeboxing as his 'T' in SMART.

How to Calculate Man Hours

Man-hours are a crucial element in submitting a winning project bid as well as charging for work completed. Because labor constitutes such a large portion of any contract work, estimating and reporting hours accurately is crucial to having a successful business.

Part 1

Estimating Man-Hours for a Project Bid

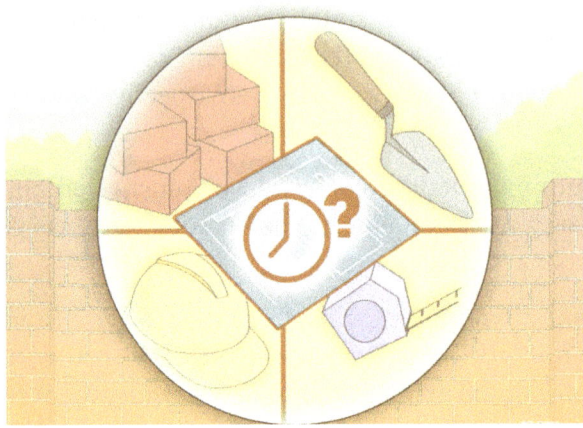

1. Divide your project into components. The first part of calculating the man-hours you will need to do a job is to split up the project into smaller components. Then estimate the amount of hours needed to complete each component. These components should be designated according to the type of labor involved. If you are building an apartment complex, you will need excavation, construction, electrical, plumbing, and so on. Make sure that every component of your project is included in the estimate.

2. Determine the type of workers you need. This largely depends on the complexity of the tasks that need to be accomplished. You don't need a foreman to do every job. Some simpler tasks can be done by assistants or apprentices. Figuring this out is harder for larger jobs that require a mix of labor to do tasks that range from simple to complex.

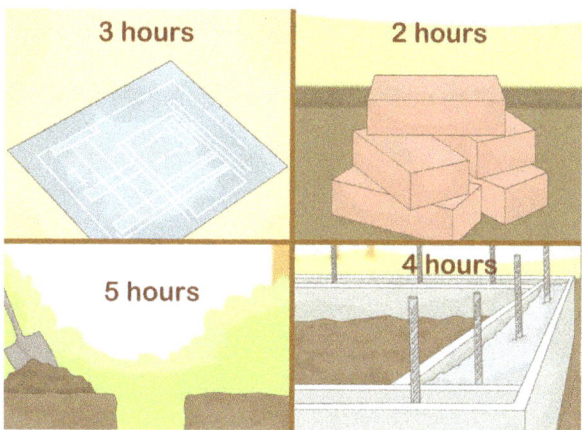

3. Estimate the time needed to complete each component. Once you have determined your components and the types of labor each requires, estimate the total number of man-hours it would take your workers to complete a step from start to finish. Do not include breaks. This number should be the hours of dedicated labor it will take to finish a step.

- If you are familiar with the type of work required in a step, you can draw from past projects to get time estimates. For example, if you know it took one worker ten hours to install four new windows, or 2.5 hours per window, your current project will likely be similar.

- If a step in your project includes a type of labor you're not familiar with, you should do some research in preparing your estimate. Depending on the project, you may be able to get valuable information online or from another contractor. You can also hire a consultant familiar with the type of labor you need. This person can help you estimate the hours required in a certain step.

- Factor in things like job difficulty when making your estimate. If the windows on your upcoming project are on the seventh story of a building, and your old project's windows were on the first story, increase your hours-per-window rate to reflect this difference.

- Include estimates for time spent on administrative tasks that may be required by the contract.

4. Include hours for supervisors. You may also include project hours for a foreman or manager, who will lead the team of workers and manage reporting details and timeline compliance. Some

projects may require more than one supervisor or foreman, managing different components of the project. Other projects may require different levels of supervision. You may have foreman managing workers in different components of the project and an overall supervisor who manages all of the foremen.

5. Use your estimates to prepare a project timeline. Your client will likely specify a time for completion of the project. Perhaps he will ask you to indicate in your bid how soon you can complete your work. You can use the steps and hours you have calculated to develop a project timeline. Determine which components can be completed simultaneously and which must be completed sequentially, where the input of one process depends upon the output of the previous process. If you know when each step of the project needs to be completed, you can divide the number of hours needed to complete a step by the number of eight-hour workdays in the time period. You may be able to extend or shorten the project timeline by adding or removing laborers. The more laborers you have, the faster you can complete a step.

- Some projects may require more than 8 hour days or 40 hours week to meet schedule. They will require overtime which should be charged to the job

- For example, if you have one month to lay the foundation of a new home, and you know the foundation requires 1000 hours of labor, divide 1000 by the number of eight-hour workdays in the month to calculate the number of laborers you need to hire to complete that step on time. (1000 project hours / 20 work days in the month = 50 hours per day; 50 hours per day / 8 hours per worker = 6.25 laborers needed.) Round the number of laborers up or down to a whole number, and adjust accordingly the number of workdays required.

- Be realistic about the number of workers you can hire in a given time period. If you need seven electricians to complete wiring in a week, this may be unrealistic, depending on the availability of electricians in your area. You may need to extend your timeline to accommodate the availability of labor for your project.

- If you plan to complete multiple steps at the same time, you'll need separate laborers to work on each step.

6. Prepare and submit your bid. Add the hours for each type of labor you need, so you have a total for each type. If you require just one type of labor, you can combine all of the project hours into one number. If you need multiple types of labor, your bid should specify the total hours for each type. You should include all labor costs including taxes and benefits. Some Federal contracts may require a minimum wage for each category of workers. Also, include any markup you plan to charge.

- As an example, imagine you have been hired to install a new kitchen in a medium-sized home. You have divided your project into steps, each requiring plumbing, electrical, and general construction work. Your bid should reflect the total electrician man-hours, plumber man-hours, and general-laborer man-hours, as well as the pay rates for each type of labor.

7. Adjust your man-hour estimates as the work progresses. Because time estimates are really just guesses, you will need to update your estimates as your project goes along. You will probably bill your client based on the actual hours your team works, so you should provide your client updated hourly estimates as time passes. This helps prevent surprises for your client when billing time rolls around.

- Include a "fudge factor," which is an increase in estimated time due to unknown causes. The amount of fudge factor depends upon the complexity of the job, availability of labor, dependence upon outside agents, and the relationship of one process to another.

- Most contractors make it clear that their bid is only an estimate, that actual hours will vary, and that clients will pay for actual hours worked as the job progresses. However, it is possible a client will want to pay you a lump sum based on your estimate and not pay for actual hours worked. Pay close attention to any contract language that would signal this kind of arrangement, as this requires very careful estimation on the part of the contractor.

- If your client will pay you based on actual hours worked, remember that your bid served as an estimate, and that you should not charge for significantly more hours than you planned unless you can cite reasonable justification. If you run into problems and know you are going to go over your time estimates, keep the client informed in order to prevent miscommunication.

- Have a written agreement that defines contingencies and out-of-scope work. Include the process for identifying and approving these changes, such as necessary approvals and documentation.

Part 2

Reporting Man Hours for Contract Jobs

1. Collect information on your workers. Maintain accurate employee files for everyone working on your project. That will include payroll records and all legally required documents. If you are using engineers, electricians, plumbers, or other licensed workers, you will need to keep on file proof of their active certifications. This is required for most engineering and construction jobs whether or not they are government contracts. It is your responsibility to ensure everyone working for you is properly certified, including subcontractors.

- You may pay people who are not your employees to do work on your project. These "subcontractors" work for you, the contractor, and you bill your client for their labor. Even though subcontractors are not actually your employees, you should gather their certification information and keep it on file. As the contractor, you are responsible for ensuring that anyone you hire to work on a project is qualified, unless otherwise specified in their contract.

- Government contracts generally require additional employee and subcontractor information indicating compliance with federal law. This may include reporting on employees' ethnicity and pay rates to ensure there is no discrimination taking place on the jobsite. If you have a government contract, read it carefully and follow all of the instructions for hiring and reporting in order to prevent difficulty in getting paid.

2. Track your workers' time. To submit accurate reports to your client, you need a reliable method of tracking how many hours your workers are on the job. You can use a time clock or a written time sheet, but these records should be verified to ensure they are accurate. Depending on your contract, you may be subject to periodic audits and may be required to prove that the hours you submit are justified.

- One way to ensure the accuracy of time reporting is to establish supervisors over each employee or employee group. At the end of the week when an employee submits his or her timecard, the supervisor can review and sign the card, certifying the information is correct. This will prevent employees from submitting time cards for hours they did not work.

- You may also consider using an electronic timecard system to track your employees' work on the job. Be sure the system is controlled to prevent abuse. You'll want to be able to prove that's the case if your hourly reporting comes under question.

- Government clients are required by law to gather all of this information before paying their contractors, because they are using taxpayer money to pay for the work. You can expect a heightened level of scrutiny when reporting time on government jobs. Carefully follow all reporting instructions detailed in your agreement.

3. Send your client payroll reports at regular intervals. Your contract should specify how often you are to report man-hours to your client in order to receive payment. When you submit these reports, you will likely transfer information from your payroll and timekeeping documents to a dedicated report for your client comparing a number of hours you are charging to the estimates you submitted during bidding. If there are large variances between your actual hours and your estimates, you will need to provide explanations of these variances to your client.

4. Use your records to prepare future estimates. At the end of a project, your time-tracking information will be extremely valuable, as it gives you details about how long it took to complete specific jobs. You can use this data to create hourly estimates, such as the number of hours per square foot of laid tile or the down time after laying fresh cement. Use this information to improve your future bids and keep your business profitable.

Tardiness (scheduling)

In scheduling, tardiness is a measure of a delay in executing certain operations and earliness is a measure of finishing operations before due time. The operations may depend on each other and on the availability of equipment to perform them.

Typical examples include job scheduling in manufacturing and data delivery scheduling in data processing networks.

In manufacturing environment, inventory management considers both tardiness and earliness undesirable. Tardiness involves backlog issues such as customer compensation for delays and loss of goodwill. Earliness incurs expenses for storage of the manufactured items.

Mathematical Formulations

In an environment with multiple jobs, let the deadline be d_i and the completion time be C_i of job i. Then for job i lateness is $L_i = C_i - d_i$, earliness is $E_i = \max\{0, d_i - C_i\}$, tardiness is $T_i = \max\{0, C_i - d_i\}$. The common objective functions are $C_{max}, L_{max}, E_{max}, T_{max}, \Sigma C_i, \Sigma L_i, \Sigma E_i, \Sigma T_i$ or weighted version of these sums, $w_i C_{max}, w_i L_{max}, w_i E_{max}, w_i T_{max}, \Sigma w_i C_i, \Sigma w_i L_i, \Sigma w_i E_i, \Sigma w_i T_i$, where every job comes with a weight w_i. The weight is a representation of job cost, priority, etc.

In a large number of cases the problems of optimizing these functions are NP-hard.

Timesheet

Contemporary time sheet

A timesheet (or time sheet) is a method for recording the amount of a worker's time spent on each job. Traditionally a sheet of paper with the data arranged in tabular format, a timesheet is now often a digital document or spreadsheet. The time cards stamped by time clocks can serve as a timesheet or provide the data to fill one. These, too, are now often digital. Timesheets came into use in the 19th century as time books.

Use

Originally developed for an employer to calculate payroll, timesheets can also be used for management accounting. Timesheets may record the start and end time of tasks or just the duration. It may contain a detailed breakdown of tasks accomplished throughout the project or program. This information may be used for payroll, client billing, and increasingly for project costing, estimation, tracking, and management.

Some companies provide web-based timesheet software or services that provide a means to track time for payroll, billing and project management. One of the major uses of timesheets in a project management environment is comparing planned costs versus actual costs, as well as measuring employee performance, and identifying problematic tasks. This knowledge can drive corporate strategy as users stop performing or reassign unprofitable work.

Time Cards

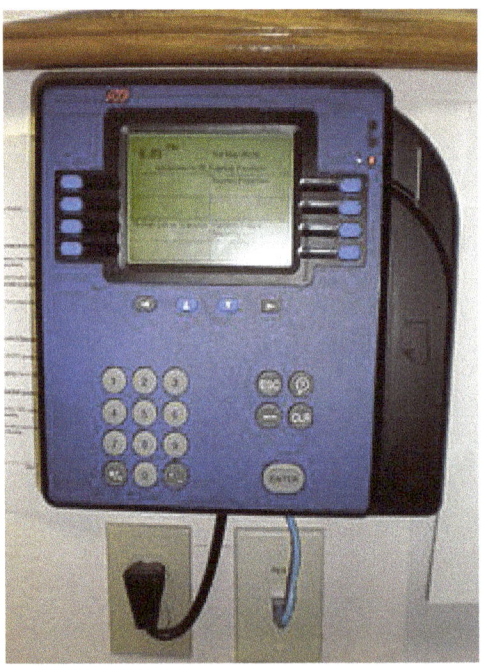

An ADP Model 4500 timecard reader

Factory workers may often have a "time card" (also known as punch card) and "punch in" by inserting their card into an automatic timestamp machine (called a time clock or bundy clock) when starting and ending their work shift, though other card technologies such as swipe cards have become more prevalent.

Advantages

Time tracking can lower costs in three ways: by making payroll processing more efficient, by making costs visible so you can lower them, and by automating billing and invoicing.

Time tracking can increase revenue through automating billing, which tends to make it easier for a company to get correct invoices out for all hours worked by consulting staff. This speeds up payment and eliminates the hassles of 'dropping' bills.

By lowering costs in three ways, and increasing revenue in one way, timesheet management technologies that are web-based can improve the health of companies.

In project management, timesheets can also be used to build a body of knowledge about how much effort tasks take to develop. Machine learning is being used to automatically find patterns in timesheets — then using this information to recommend more accurate project plans in the future. For example, if developing a training plan has historically taken a month, then it can be assumed that creating a new one will take a month. Also, most timesheet software has the ability to track resource costs and project expenses to allow for better future budgeting.

For the HR function, the time spent on activities by individuals can be analyzed over a period of time and categorized into broad types. Based on the outcome roles could be realigned.

Time-tracking Software

Time-tracking software is a category of computer software that allows its users to record time spent on tasks. This software is used by employees and employers in many industries, including hourly workers and also professionals who bill their customers by the hour, such as lawyers, freelancers and accountants. It can be used together with multiple other tools like project management software, customer support and accounting to name just a few. It is an electronic version of the traditional paper timesheet. Tracking time can increase productivity, as businesses can better understand what practices lead to wasted time. This type of software encourages accountability for large businesses, and allows business owners to keep all time data in a central location which allows easier data analysis by human resources departments. Features offered by time-tracking software include:

- Automatic generation of invoices to the professional's clients or customers based on the time spent.

- Additional billing of related costs to each client or file.

- workforce management packages that include time and attendance, scheduling, absence management, human resources, payroll, talent management, and labor analytics.

Types of Time-tracking Software

Timesheet

> Allows users to manually enter time spent on tasks.

Time-tracking/recording

> Automatically records activities performed on a computer.

Time-tracking software can be:

- Standalone: Used only to record timesheets and generate reports.

- Integrated as part of:

    o Accounting systems, e.g. timesheet data fed directly to company accounts.

    o Billing systems, e.g. to generate invoices, especially for contractors, lawyers, etc.

    o Project management systems, e.g. timesheet data used by project management software to visualize the effort being spent on projects or tasks.

    o Payroll systems, e.g. to pay employees based on time worked.

    o Resource scheduling, e.g. bi-directional integration allows schedulers to schedule staff to tasks, which, once complete, can be confirmed and converted to timesheets.

Timesheet Software

Timesheet software is software used to maintain timesheets. It was popularized when computers were first introduced to the office environment with the goal of automating heavy paperwork for big organizations. Timesheet software allows entering time spent performing different tasks.

When used within companies, employees enter the time they've spent on tasks into electronic timesheets. These timesheets can then be approved or rejected by supervisors or project managers.

Since 2006, timesheet software has been moving to mobile platforms (smartphones, tablets, smart watches, etc.) enabling better tracking of employees whose work involves multiple locations.

Time-tracking/recording Software

Time-tracking/recording software automates the time-tracking process by recording the activities performed on a computer and the time spent on each of them. This software is intended to be an improvement over timesheet software. Its goal is to offer a general picture of computer usage. Automatic time-tracking/recording software records and shows the usage of applications, documents, games, websites, etc.

When used within companies, this software allows monitoring the productivity of employees by recording the tasks they perform on their computers. It can be used to help filling out timesheets.

The American Payroll Association estimates that companies can save 2% of gross payroll costs each year by automating time tracking.

When used by freelancers, this software helps to create reports for clients (e.g. timesheets and invoices) or to prove work that was done.

Time-tracking Methods

There are several ways companies track employee time using time tracking software.

Durational

> Employees enter the duration of the task but not the times when it was performed.

Chronological

> Employees enter start and end times for the task.

Automatic

> The system automatically calculates time spent on tasks or whole projects, using a connected device or a personal computer, and user input using start and stop buttons. Users can retrieve logged tasks and view the duration, or the start and stop times.

Exception-based

> The system automatically records standard working hours except for approved time off or LOA.

Clock-in clock-out

> Employees manually record arrival and departure times.

Monitoring

> The system records active and idle time of employees. It might also record screen captures.

Location-based

> The system determines the working status of employees based on their location.

- Resource-scheduling: by scheduling resources in advance, employees schedules can be easily converted to timesheets.

How to Consider a Time Tracking Device for Project Manager

In a design, it is imperative that the project handler all together with the assistance of his team create and work out a plan schedule and timetable. Holding a plan schedule will supply an introduction on how far a project is anticipated to function before it can be rank and presented.

Steps

1. Create and work out a plan schedule and timetable. In a design, it is imperative that the project handler all together with the assistance of his team create and work out a plan schedule and timetable.

- Holding a plan schedule will supply an introduction on how far a project is anticipated to function before it can be rank and presented. This would also help in distinguishing the factors that may as a matter of fact hit the design's progress and estimate the number of time thought necessary to fulfill the job, the design's monetary budget, the survival of team members with the obligatory skill set and the assets essential to complete the design.

2. Know time supervision. It was stated that, once a project is well on its way, and a schedule is formulated, one of the superior obligations of a design director is time supervision. He should be efficient to track time on how long does a section or a person in his group requires to fulfill a special assignment. Tasks or responsibilities that are given to team members are usually straight or hierarchical. This symbolizes that the end of special job is the root of another.

- Every task is dependent with each other; therefore if single job is not accomplished in time, it would drive a delay of the starting of the subsequent obligation in the hierarchy. A domino impression will follow as the slowing of a task would pose prospective risks, extra costs and deficit of resources. It would likewise put some members of the group who are expecting the completion of the obligation before them to wait idly. Portion of programming should as well be the apportioning of time for contingency programmes in case a hazard beyond the design's control is experienced.

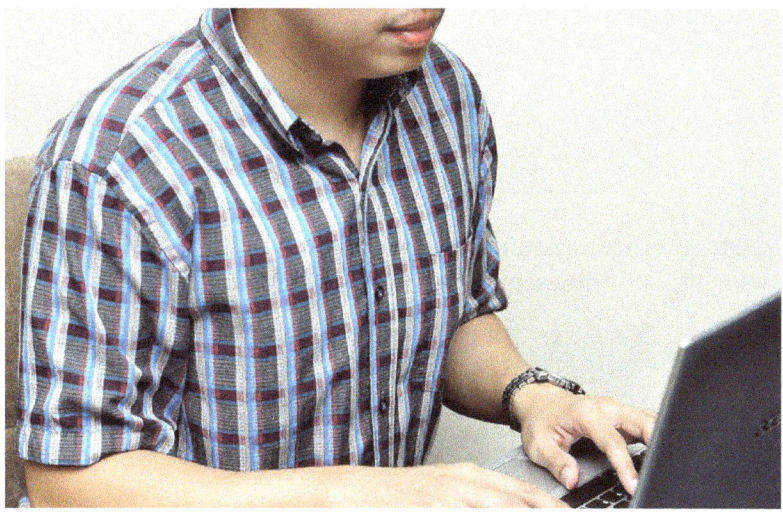

3. Monitor the growth. Time monitoring is really essential to the victory of the project as it will be of aid in lessening the possibilities of the domino outcome expressed above. If a project managing director is efficient to monitor the growth, he would be efficient to pinpoint what problems needs to be addressed and what can be set apart at a subsequent time. He would as well be provided with a bird's eye see of how the project is progressing, well discovering procedures that can be cleared upon on or moved out. He will likewise be efficient to look if his team is working in agreement to the schedule that they have organized.

- The practice of a time tracking software will as well assist in studying the project's weekly work flow, giving the plan handler a large breakdown of the schedule, correcting it each time the need arises. Web handling computer software is also a natural way to time track a plan. Carrying the data online would not only be advantageous to the design manager but it will also empower the team with the capability to monitor each other's progresses in a and schedule and simultaneously offering the customers with an up to date report.

How to use the Talygen Time Tracker

The first step towards good time management is to understand where it goes. Although few will admit, not all time spent in front of the computer screen is equally productive. Few people have an idea of how many hours in office are wasted checking emails and watching cat videos. Time tracking can help you to keep track, by using the Talygen Time Tracker, to be more productive at work.

Steps

1. Double click on the tracker icon. You may find it in Downloads or Desktop. You can also use the search function in your PC (Windows and Linux) or Mac locate the tracker.

2. Enter your username and password that you created during registration and click on LOGIN. This image uses a dummy username (johnsmith@talygen.com) and password.

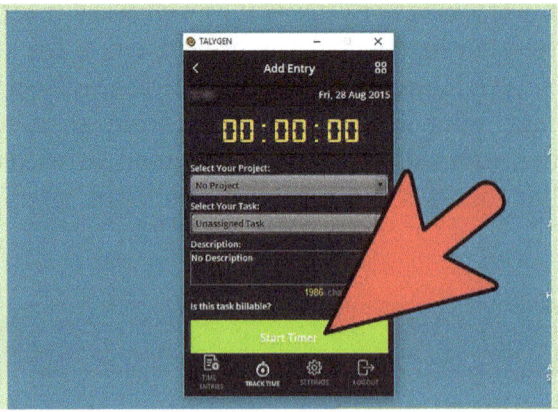

3. Click on START TIMER to enter a tracking session. If you username and password are correct, you will be greeted by the home screen. The tracker shows you six options: SYNC, START TIMER, Home Button, Start Time, Settings, and Logout. SYNC and START TIMER are near the top. The remaining four functions are shown as four icons at the bottom.

- SYNC: Clicking on SYNC synchronizes the data collected on your tracker to the data in the Talygen cloud.

- START TIMER: Takes you to a new screen, where you can select a project.

- Home Button: Is to be used when you want to return to the home screen.

- Start Timer: Same as START TIMER.

- Settings: Personalizes your tracker. You may need admin privileges to make changes.

- Logout: Is used to logs out of the tracker. It is normally used when you are finished with the day's work.

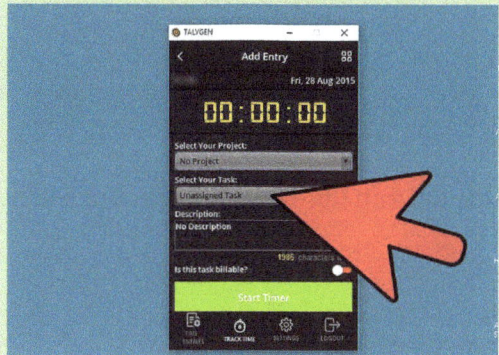

4. Click on START TIMER after you have entered a project, task, description, and marked the project as billable or non-billable.

- No Project Dropdown Menu: Click on the No Project dropdown menu to pick a project.

- Unassigned Task: Use this function to select a subtask you will work on.

- No Description: Mention the details of your work.

- Is this task billable?: Selecting "On" shows the client is paying for the work you are about to do, and "Off" shows you are not going to be paid for work. For instance, click on "On" if you are a programmer and about to start app development. Select "Off" if you are reading emails and browsing YouTube.

5. You are actively tracking time now. Use PAUSE, STOP, and UPDATE to control tracking.

- PAUSE: Pauses the tracker.

- STOP: To be used when you are finished with your task.

- UPDATE: Used to switch between tasks.

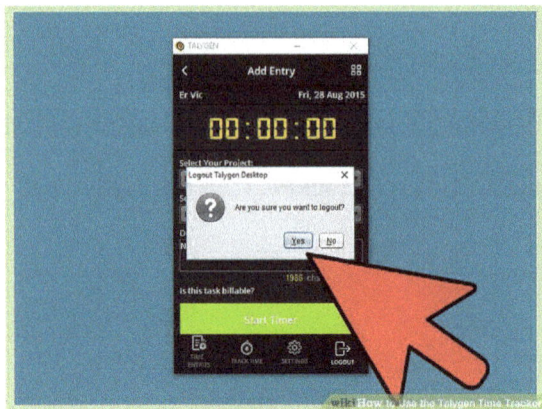

6. Click on Logout when it's time to wrap up. The tracking data will be synced with your company's Talygen cloud.

Time and Attendance

Time and attendance systems (TNA) are used to track and monitor when employees start and stop work. A time and attendance system provides many benefits to organizations as it enables an employer to have full control of their employees working hours as it monitors late arrivals, early departures, time taken on breaks and absenteeism. It also helps to control labor costs by reducing over-payments, which are often caused by paying employees for time that are not working, and eliminates transcription error, interpretation error and intentional error. TNA systems are also invaluable for ensuring compliance with labor regulations regarding proof of attendance. All of these benefits provide both employer and employees with confidence in the accuracy of their wage payments all while improving productivity.

Manual Systems

Traditionally manual systems were used that rely on highly skilled people laboriously adding up paper cards which have times stamped onto them using a time stamping machine such as the Bundy Clock. Time stamping machines were used for over a century but have since been phased out and replaced with cheaper automated systems which eliminate the need for payroll staff to manually input employee hours.

Automated Systems

Modern automated time and attendance systems simply require employees to touch or swipe to identify themselves and record their working hours as they enter or leave the work area. Originally this consisted of using a RFID electronic tag or a barcode badge but these have been replaced by bio-metrics (vein reader, hand geometry, fingerprint, or facial recognition), and touch screens devices. Modern biometric TNA systems offer additional benefits over traditional manual systems which include

- Faster processing of employees as attendance can be recorded with just one touch or a quick scan

- Fraud prevention by eliminating duplicate and fake registration

- Saves time as attendance can either be integrated directly with your payroll system or it can produce a report that can be downloaded or printed

- Improves punctuality and reduces long breaks and absenteeism

- Saves time as it can either integrate directly with your payroll system or produce a report that can be downloaded or printed.

Permissions

All chapters in this book are published with permission under the Creative Commons Attribution Share Alike License or equivalent. Every chapter published in this book has been scrutinized by our experts. Their significance has been extensively debated. The topics covered herein carry significant information for a comprehensive understanding. They may even be implemented as practical applications or may be referred to as a beginning point for further studies.

We would like to thank the editorial team for lending their expertise to make the book truly unique. They have played a crucial role in the development of this book. Without their invaluable contributions this book wouldn't have been possible. They have made vital efforts to compile up to date information on the varied aspects of this subject to make this book a valuable addition to the collection of many professionals and students.

This book was conceptualized with the vision of imparting up-to-date and integrated information in this field. To ensure the same, a matchless editorial board was set up. Every individual on the board went through rigorous rounds of assessment to prove their worth. After which they invested a large part of their time researching and compiling the most relevant data for our readers.

The editorial board has been involved in producing this book since its inception. They have spent rigorous hours researching and exploring the diverse topics which have resulted in the successful publishing of this book. They have passed on their knowledge of decades through this book. To expedite this challenging task, the publisher supported the team at every step. A small team of assistant editors was also appointed to further simplify the editing procedure and attain best results for the readers.

Apart from the editorial board, the designing team has also invested a significant amount of their time in understanding the subject and creating the most relevant covers. They scrutinized every image to scout for the most suitable representation of the subject and create an appropriate cover for the book.

The publishing team has been an ardent support to the editorial, designing and production team. Their endless efforts to recruit the best for this project, has resulted in the accomplishment of this book. They are a veteran in the field of academics and their pool of knowledge is as vast as their experience in printing. Their expertise and guidance has proved useful at every step. Their uncompromising quality standards have made this book an exceptional effort. Their encouragement from time to time has been an inspiration for everyone.

The publisher and the editorial board hope that this book will prove to be a valuable piece of knowledge for students, practitioners and scholars across the globe.

Index